ALABASTER JARS

Life in Abundance

Collection 2

Edited and Compiled by

Fylvia Fowler Kline

ISBN: 061591909X
ISBN-13: 978-0615919096

Unless otherwise noted, all scriptural references are taken from The Message.

Dedication

To the first 100 women in Nepal who learned how to
read because of the sale of Alabaster Jars
and the work of Interra Foundation.

May each of you be the instrument of change in your
village, your neighborhood, your family and in the life
of every little girl you know.

Table of Contents

vi

Acknowledgements

Everyone has a story to tell—a story that is not just
therapeutic to the storyteller, but one that inspires
someone somewhere who hears that story.

I am thankful for the 35 women who join me in telling
our stories in this second collection of Alabaster Jars.
Some of them I've known forever, some I've never
met in person; but all of whom I consider friends.

Foreword

Looking at us, you wouldn't have pegged us as friends. I was older with adolescent children; Melinda had two little boys, one still in diapers. I was a control freak; she mellow and creative. But being two strangers in an even stranger land with workaholic husbands, we were drawn to each other and became the best of friends in the worst of times. We were *sathis*.

Sathi is the Nepali word for *friends. But it* has a much broader connotation and means more than friends. It's the same word used for both *friend* and *spouse*, and refers to more than hanging out and doing fun stuff together. Sathis are faithful, dependable partners with an eternal bond that can never be broken. Nothing—not distance, not time, not even death—allows me to desathi or unfriend Melinda. I have not seen her in at least a decade, but should I need her for anything, she will be there. This I know without a doubt.

The contributors of this book are sathis. Most of us have never met one another. None of us are making any money from this book. But all of us are sathis through a bond and shared passion to teach women in developing countries how to read and write. Our desire is for all women to be literate. Through the power of literacy, the women we help will be able to understand events happening around them, travel and shop by themselves, help their children with homework, make decisions on their own. With the ability to read and write comes freedom and independence—the right of every human being.

One hundred percent of the proceeds from the sale of this book funds women's literacy programs through InterraFoundation.org.

Read the book. Be blessed. And be a sathi by contributing to the next portion of *Alabaster Jars*. You don't have to be a published writer; just tell us your story and help bring independence and freedom of expression to all women.

Fylvia Fowler Kline, November 2013

* Submissions for the next portion of Alabaster Jars are being accepted online at alabasterjars.org

The Horse Before the Cart

I am God, your God, who brought you out of the land of Egypt, out of a life of slavery. Exodus 20:1, 2

By the first chapter of Exodus, several hundred years and a few generations have passed since Israel's bondage had begun. That's a long time to be in a foreign land. Strange customs, strange gods; pretty much everything is unfamiliar and different.

After the first couple of decades, the lines were getting blurred—traditions were being forgotten, promises broken and fuzzy compromises made. They were only human, without a leader and probably feeling very detached from a once tangible God.

So when God and Moses paired up to lead them out of bondage and into the Promised Land, I imagine they needed an intense orientation session to rediscover their identity—to figure out who they were, where they were going and what they were called to do. Hence the 40 years of wilderness wanderings were the lessons in *I am Your God 101*.

The exodus from Egypt to Canaan makes a lot of sense when you look at it from this perspective. Yet what impresses me the most about this story is what happens in chapter 20 when God finally spells out the terms of the contract between His people and Him.

He could have handed out copies of the Ten Commandments the night the people of Israel left Egypt. Perhaps the tablets could have been carved into each dining table as families gathered to eat the meal of unleavened bread. Or maybe He could have inserted a copy into every packed bag that stood in the bloodstained foyer, ready for the journey. Or tattooed it on their forearms. That night of grand departure was the perfect time for God to hand out His policies and procedures, His do's and don'ts. That would certainly have eliminated the chapter after chapter of bad decisions, misunderstandings and a whole lot of whining.

Yet God waited 19 long chapters before He chiseled His law into stone. This long wait says so much about our God. Before He gave them the Law on Sinai, God rescued them from slavery. Before God expected obedience, God poured out his saving grace.

In God's order of things, His grace is the horse that comes before the cart. His grace is the force that pulls us into salvation.

_____

by Fylvia Fowler Kline

The Right Job, the Right Time

You, O God, know every one of us inside and out. Make plain which of these two men you choose to take the place in this ministry. Acts 1:24.

I had just interviewed within a church organization. I really wanted the position. I prayed I'd get the job, if I were meant to have it. Those hiring for the position were also praying; they wanted God's help in finding the right person.

As I prayed, I was reminded of the 11 in the upper room. The men had just been through a wringer of emotional events: Jesus' death on the cross, His resurrection from the tomb and then His ascension into heaven. It had been a tumultuous two months.

I imagine the apostles gathered together, confused and overwhelmed. I picture them clinging to Jesus' words. The fate of Christianity rested upon their shoulders. As they defined apostleship, they knew that it was time to choose a replacement for Judas. Surely, Matthias and Joseph both had worthy attributes. It would have been easy to follow human logic and obvious qualifications as their criteria. Instead, they prayer in earnest and in submission: *Make plain which of these two men you choose.*

6

God chose Matthias.

There is great peace in allowing God to lead in our lives. Although I really wanted the job, I wanted even more God's will to be done. We have a tendency to pray for things that are not in our best interest, and we are devastated when God says *No* or seemingly fails to answer.

He does see the future, and He knows whether something will bless us or hinder us. Sometimes, as in Matthias' case, God says *Yes*. At other times, as in my desire for this certain job, God says *No*. As we draw close to Him, we are more and more able to accept disappointments.

If today you are awaiting an answer, be comforted knowing God has already answered your prayer—in His perfect time!

---

by Tonya Mechling

Twice Fallen

Quickly I picked myself up from the sidewalk and assessed the damage. The sidewalk was fine except for the crack I just tripped over. I, however, was bleeding profusely from my chin and lower lip. Plus my right arm was crooked and my lower jaw was no longer aligned with its upper counterpart.

Fast forward to the emergency room. The bleeding had stopped, but I still looked frightful. My clothes and white walking shoes were stained with blood and my lip was swelling. *When will it be our turn?* my husband and I wondered out loud several times.

Finally, my name was called and we were escorted to an examining room. We welcomed the relative quiet of this cubicle and the attentiveness of the physician's assistant and nurse. Calmly they stitched the wounds on my chin and lip. Gently they delivered me to the technicians who did the x-rays and CAT scans. And with just the right measure of sympathy, they gave us the results and told us what we needed to do and who we needed to see the next day. And so with prescriptions for pain meds in hand, my husband and I stood up to leave.

Wait! Wait just a minute! Sit back down! the nurse instructed us as she picked up a towel and basin and went to the sink for water.

Now what? my husband and I both looked at each other, wondering. But we did as we were told.

Balancing the basin in both hands, she walked over to me and knelt at my feet. Slowly, methodically, she began to cleanse my shoes of blood. Slowly they became white again, while the water became red.

My eyes welled up with tears.

We are all twice fallen. We are all born into sin. We cannot escape or deny it. And because we are born into sin, we will think sinful thoughts and commit sinful acts. But at some point, Jesus calls out to us, *Wait! Wait just a minute!* Then He invites us to sit down. And when we do, He'll fill a basin with water, kneel at our feet, and with His own garment, He'll wash us clean, while His own hands and clothes become stained with our blood, our sins.

Yes, we are all twice fallen. But with Jesus there is no waiting in crowded, noisy emergency rooms. *Come unto me,* He calls (Matt. 11:28, NIV). And when we turn in the direction of His voice, there He stands, holding a basin and a towel, ready and longing to make us clean with His blood.

----

by Lyndelle Brower Chiomenti

The What If's

Trust God from the bottom of your heart; don't try to figure out everything on your own. Listen for God's voice in everything you do, everywhere you go; he's the one who will keep you on track. Proverbs 3: 5, 6

I never had a relationship with the Lord. Always independent and strong, my life by 48 had been difficult. Attempts to trust people had always ended in disappointment and new fears piled on top of old ones. With every experience, my heart hardened even more.

Yet, somewhere in the recesses of my heart, I had not completely let go of hope. And the Lord knew this. With divine, covert operations, He'd plant a small *what if* in my heart that I'd end up pursuing. I would always follow them to the end result, no matter what. And trust me, the devil threw in a great many of his *what if's* too!

One of those *what if's* in 2006 gave me a husband. I met my husband through a discussion of Jesus. Every morning I would race to my computer in Chicago and he to his in Oregon. I would type my question of the day about the Lord and Michael would answer. The *what if's* would pour out of my hardened heart, and

God and Michael together would help me see the answer.

A whirlwind romance had me marrying this man four short months later over a *what if I didn't?* I moved to Oregon because of a relationship that helped me find the Lord. But somehow, I still couldn't fully trust Him. Every day was a struggle, yet every day brought me that much more comfortable to turn my life over completely to God.

God has not disappointed me yet. He has helped Michael and me through battles over cancer, finances and so much more. Through it all, my heart has remained softened. And I know for certain that I can face whatever *what if* that comes my way with a courage I never had before.

---

by Laurie Owen

Toast on Pretty Plate

If toast were a conversation starter, it would be the drably simple, *Hi.*

Toast is my obligatory, minimum dietary sustenance. When I am too busy, too sick or too tired to sit down for a satisfying meal, I have toast. Similarly, *Hi* is my obligatory, minimum social interaction. When I am too busy, too impatient or simply can't be bothered to care about anybody, I say *Hi* and keep going.

Both these obligatory minimums were completely obliterated with the epiphany I had whilst unpacking my precious stack of mismatched china: Years of random scavenging through garage sales have yielded me a pretty assortment of china, tea towels and knick knacks. I never pay more than a dollar for anything, so I really shouldn't be so stingy in my use of them. But I am. I store them safely in the corner of the tallest shelf in my pantry, cushioned by sheets of newspaper. And the only time I touch them is when I clean the shelf or move from one home to another.

Such a waste. I should be enjoying these pretty little things, I said to myself as I unpacked the box of china yet again in yet another move. It's no big deal if one breaks. A few dimes under my sofa cushions and a sunny Sunday at a flea market will surely get me several more. Perhaps ones even prettier.

My china reminded me of my words. It's a gift I'm told I have–People, strangers even, often tell me their darkest secrets and despairs with great ease. And I seem to always find the right words to say. Yet I don't enjoy these interactions and avoid them with a hurried *Hi*. Instead of being generous with my words, I stash them on an emotionally-detached shelf for use only in emergencies.

That's just bad. Wasteful. I really should couch my *Hi* in a mouthful of words that express genuine interest.

With that, I decided to dress up both my toast and my greeting.

With that epiphany, I sat my too-tired self down for a bare minimum of dietary sustenance on a pretty white plate filigreed in French blue. And vowed to take the time to say more than *Hi*.

My toast never tasted so good :)

---

by Fylvia Fowler Kline

The Cat and the Turkey

I will never leave thee, nor forsake thee. Hebrews 13:5, KJV.

My Thanksgiving began with me feeling sort of blue. Then my cat got sick and I was very blue. I didn't want to be driving my cat to the vet when I had plans to cook Thanksgiving dinner.

Trying to make the most of the day, I figured I could still squeeze in some quick shopping after a visit to the vet. But then came the unexpected bill. After labs and medicine, I had nothing left for groceries to fix my Thanksgiving dinner! My bank account would be zero until my next paycheck on Monday. I cried all the way home feeling even worse, yet still grateful for many things—the cat that was going to be okay, my daughter who was waiting for me at home, friends and family whom I loved. I did have so much for which to be thankful; dinner should not matter so much. In fact, my daughter also assured me that it was no big deal. But for some reason I couldn't stop feeling so blue about the turkey that wasn't on my table.

Unable to shake off the blues, I plopped down to browse Craigslist. And there it was, an ad posted just minutes earlier: *Are you truly thankful today? The*

14

first person to email and tell us what you are thankful for gets a free Butterball turkey.

I quickly emailed a response about my cat and the trip to the vet. I not only got the turkey but also some fixings! I giggled all the way home, with the turkey next to me. My blues were nowhere in sight as I was overwhelmed by my God's presence that day. He was there right through my blues and knew just how to fix it.

But He wasn't done. A few minutes later, I got an email from my bank: Turns out that my employer deposited my paycheck earlier than usual. I could now go shopping after all and get all the groceries needed to make a proper Thanksgiving meal!

That evening, I sent out emails bragging about my wonderful Jesus.

Coincidentally, the turkey weighed exactly as much as my cat—11.9 pounds!

by Kathy Walling

How do We Serve?

If words, let it be God's words; if help, let it be God's hearty help. That way, God's bright presence will be evident in everything through Jesus, and he'll get all the credit as the One mighty in everything—encores to the end of time. Oh, yes! I Peter 4:11

For me, the story of the prodigal son always concludes with the reactions of three people: the father running and hugging his filthy, bedraggled son; the prodigal son remorseful, afraid and unsure of his father's reaction to his return; and the older brother terribly unhappy about his father's unbelievable, forgiving spirit. Even as a child, every time I heard the story or saw it reenacted, it ended the same way — with three people reacting in three different ways.

Recently though, I've been thinking about the servant who brings the special robe and gold ring for the father to put on the prodigal son. What kind of servant was he? Did he carry tales to the older son of how the father was celebrating his son's return? Did he scoff inwardly at the repentant son? Or was he happy that the son had returned and was honored to be the one carrying the clothes and ring? Did he try to pacify the older brother? Did he perform his duties to his best abilities?

Not all of us are chosen to play primary roles in life. Some are sometimes called to be just servants. The servant is never recognized and forever remains on the sidelines, tucked between the curtain and center stage.

When chosen to be a servant, how do you perform your assigned tasks? Does your attitude reflect gratitude or resentment? Does your role fuel resolutions or ignite ill feelings?

by Alvina Kullu Sulankey

The Unlocked Door

Look at me. I stand at the door. I knock. Revelation 3:20

I hung Jesus on the cross and crucified Him. I did this with my adulterous choices.

It doesn't matter now what took place in our home that brought me to my choice. The bottom line is that I chose to break my contract with my God.

I made the decision to sin. I couldn't blame anyone but me. I felt so alone, so helpless, so lost. I felt God had turned His back on me. I was so ashamed. I wondered, *Is there any hope for me now? Any forgiveness? What have I done!*

For 27 years I had been living in the protection and safety of a Christian community and family. No matter where I went, I was with family, a wonderful safety net. Very involved in church and school, my faith and family were my life. So what happened?

Simply put, I took God's love for granted. I had the front door of my heart locked and guarded, but had left the back door unlocked. And it didn't take Satan long to find his way in. I lost everything. My home, my children, my husband, my in-laws, my church family, my friends and my self-respect. I felt totally worthless because most of all, I lost God and His salvation.

I had given up, but my friend Karen didn't give up on me. I didn't answer the phone or door because of my humiliation. But she was persistent. She encouraged me without being judgmental. After a while I started going back to church. I'd go in late and slip in the back pew and leave before the closing song.

Slowly it dawned on me. God didn't leave me; I left Him! He was still right there, knocking at my heart's door. All I had to do was let Him in. Colossians 1:13,14 says *God rescued us from dead-end alleys and dark dungeons. He's set us up in the kingdom of the Son he loves so much, the Son who got us out of the pit we were in, got rid of the sins we were doomed to keep repeating*

There WAS hope for me. I cried, I laughed, I repented. And I was forgiven. Once again I am in God's fold, no longer the lost sheep. I am now much more aware of Satan's snares. My relationship with God has deepened. Jesus has become my best friend. But sometimes in the dark of night I still cry because of what I did to Jesus and my family. And God reminds me that He rejoices when the lost have been found (Luke 15:32).

No matter how big your problem or sin, God is at the door knocking. I pray you will let Him in.

---

by Shianna Paxton

The Cure for Grumpiness

The clock was saying 3:33 p.m.

I saw no good omen in the triple three play. I saw nothing optimistic about three-fourths of my day at work behind me. I saw no reason to focus on the joy of soon going home to cat and husband.

All I knew was that my contract designer was late—again. And my deadline was staring at me.

I. Was. Grumpy.

It's taken me years to embrace the logic that it's futile to get mad or grumpy or sad or whatever about things over which I have no control. Ergo, the designer was no excuse to be grumpy.

But grumpy I was.

So I figured I'd walk off my grumpiness. Within 10 minutes of walking, I quickly discovered that walking in high heels only makes the grumpy even grumpier. So I headed back to my office.

Stopping at Luci's desk on my way back, I vented about my inability to shake off my grumpiness. She only added to my mood by emphasizing that I was in a pretty sorry state if I couldn't see the benefits of exercise to mood enhancement. To her credit, she did—at the end—ask me what would help eradicate my grumpy mood.

Chocolate, I responded.

And chocolate Luci had. Dark, Dove chocolate squares. One of my favorites.

Blessing her silently with twins within the next 12 months (Hope she appreciates this as much as I did the chocolate), I snarkily said, *Perhaps Dove has a witty saying that will lift my spirits.*

Back at my desk, I unwrapped my chocolate. And this was the message on the silvery inside: *Chocolate won't let you down.*

How's that for a daily dose of miracle for an underserving grump?

_____

by Fylvia Fowler Kline

Heavenly Hug

When he was still a long way off, his father saw him. His heart pounding, he ran out, embraced him, and kissed him. Luke 15:20

I'm not going to lie; I prefer not to be touched. I have a large personal space bubble and wish everyone would stay outside of it. I'm that person who will physically step away from you when you step in for a welcoming hug. It's not that I don't like being around people. I have wonderful friends and enjoy spending time with them. I just think handshakes, hugs and *air kissing* are completely unnecessary. Oh, and yes, I have read all the research on how beneficial human touch is, how healing the power of touch can be. It just doesn't work for me. But I do have one exception to this rule.

One weekend a year, two of my childhood girlfriends and I spend time laughing, crying, bragging and nourishing each other's souls. Upon arrival at this event, each participant, which means me too, is given a hug by those who have been waiting for their arrival. Under normal circumstances I would display my large can of pepper spray and demand everyone stand back 30 feet. But you see I have this friend, she shows such genuine happiness and warmth at seeing me again. When she wraps her arms around me, all my anxiety disappears. For that moment she makes me feel like she has been waiting all year for me to arrive.

When I dream of heaven and seeing Jesus for the first time, I know how His arms wrapped around me will feel. For that moment He will make me feel like He has been waiting all that time just for me to arrive. All my anxiety and sadness will be gone and replaced with the deep, soul-healing love of Jesus.

My prayer for you is that you have a friend that greets you with a heavenly hug.

_____

by Cynthia Ward

The Dentist's Office

I was at the dentist's office waiting for my son. I had a book to read, but I kept getting distracted by the people coming in. First was a man in his early 30's, sporting a bright purple Mohawk and multiple piercings on his face. I couldn't help myself; I stared— just for a couple of seconds.

Then came a deaf teenager with his mother. They sat in the corner and seemed to be arguing in sign language. I couldn't help myself; I stared—just for a couple of seconds.

Next, a young couple. She was very pregnant and didn't have a wedding band on her finger. What I really noticed was her dirty feet slipped in well-worn flip-flops. I couldn't help myself; I stared—just for a couple of seconds.

I wondered about each of them and their stories. It's so easy to weave a story with outer appearances. Yet more often what's on the inside does not match the outside. I should know better. Many times I've championed the plight of the homeless and the downtrodden with the verse, *God judges persons differently than humans do. Men and women look at*

24

the face; God looks into the heart (1 Samuel 16:7).
And yet, there I was on the brink of judgment.

Jesus loves the purple Mohawks, the dirty feet and the argumentative teens just as much as He loves me. He gives His grace freely and equally.

Was I exhibiting grace by staring and letting my mind wander? As I let my mind wander, one by one, each one in the waiting room was called to the back. I found myself alone again. As I started to beat myself up about my judgmental attitude, I remembered that it was not too late to be more like Christ. So I prayed for each of whom I had stared. I prayed that they find God's grace if they had not already.

Oddly, the Mohawk, the teen and the pregnant woman all left the dentist's office before my son came out. Even odder, they all smiled at me before they left.

My son left the dentist's office with cleaner teeth and I left with a more grace-filled soul. Three people touched me, though they never knew it. I won't waste it. I will pass it on.

_____

by Kristin Bridgman

Bobby Pin Frazzle

You don't have to know me. You just have to see me—once—to understand my eternal need for a steady supply of bobby pins.

And so, very early in our marriage, my very thoughtful husband bought me this gorgeous antique, cobalt blue jar to hold my bobby pins. This jar has traveled around the world with me and always sits to the right of my bathroom sink.

Every morning of every day, all these years, I search through my jar of bobby pins. I spend at least 20 seconds every day searching for one that has not lost its tip, its color or its grip. This means I've spent about 40 hours of my life sorting through a cobalt jar for reliable, sturdy bobby pins.

What a colossal waste of time, right? Especially, when it didn't have to be like this. If only I had taken the time to throw the bad ones in the trash. It's simply the logical thing to do. But no, I've wasted 40 hours of my life—just because I never take the time to clean out my jar, because I've never been frazzled enough by the stuff in my cobalt blue jar that didn't belong.

Life's sort of like that. We put up with stuff that should not be, that don't belong, simply because we can't be bothered to take the time to get rid of the mess. And in the process of not caring enough to set things right, we lose so much.

Guess what I finally did today? Yup, I cleaned out my cobalt jar. Here's a sampling of what I found—a key that opens nothing, a penny that isn't very special, a kernel of unpopped corn, and a bunch of misshapen, useless bobby pins.

by Fylvia Fowler Kline

True Belief

Belief is powerful. Regardless of whether your faith is placed on something true or false, a wholehearted belief in it can bring one immeasurable assurance.

Convictions affect actions; decisions prove confidence. The choices we make every day, in every situation, point in the direction of our faith.

True belief is not measured in mere words, but in deeds. I recently watched a show about a woman who is a doomsday prepper. Every aspect of her life is noticeably impacted by her belief in the soon-coming breakdown of life and government. She believes that within the next couple of years—because of the economic recession, big government and limited resources—society will break down, martial law will be enforced and general chaos will ensue.

In an effort to make ready for the impending collapse of society, she has spent $30,000 in just one year to stockpile food, create emergency escape plans, learn to use different types of weapons, buy guns and make survival kits. Her belief in this impending disaster has propelled her to be prepared to leave her home and head for the hills at a moment's notice.

Besides training herself and gathering stuff she will need, she lives in a continued state of preparedness: She never leaves home without survival gear. She spends at least six hours a day in some form of preparatory activity.

Not only is she prepared, she also works towards preparing others. She holds meetings to convince her friends of the validity of her theory.

Everything she does centers around her belief. Her checkbook, activities, home, car, pantry, lifestyle and relationships (or lack thereof) testify to her convictions; they speak of where her trust lies.

Shouldn't that be true of us as Christians? Our checkbooks, activities, homes, cars, pantries, lifestyles and relationships should reflect our beliefs, expose the true foundation of our lives.

by Deidra Manning

Walking Among Possibilities

Permanence, perseverance and persistence in spite of all obstacles, discouragements, and impossibilities: It is this that in all things distinguishes the strong soul from the weak.—Thomas Carlyle

Sitting in a crowded waiting room this past week, I watched a very young girl make her way slowly across the room. Tears pooled in my eyes at the thought that this crippled child would have to use crutches for the rest of her life. But she wasn't the least bit sad. From the sweet, careless smile which lit her innocent face, it was quite obvious that she didn't give her legs a second thought.

I was reminded of William Pitt, a British politician, who was an extremely influential figure during the French Revolution. What Pitt lacked in physical strength, he more than made up with determination. The concept of limitation was foreign to him. He never let his crutches get in the way.

Though he rarely delegated duty, he had at some point during the war given a direct command to one of his officials. When the man balked at the impossibility of the task, Pitt reprimanded him by pointing to his own crutches and confidently declared: *Sir, I walk upon impossibilities!*

There is no question that all of humanity face difficulty and hardship. Life holds much uncertainty and little hope. With God, however, there is hope because with God all things are possible (Matthew 19:26).

Whatever you are going through right now, remember that we may all lose a few battles, but we will most assuredly win the war. Now is not the time to give in to discouragement; there is too much work to do. It may be difficult, but let us all rise to the challenge.

Marie Curie summarized this well: *Life is not easy for any of us. But what of that . . . . We must believe that we are gifted for something, and that this thing, at whatever cost, must be attained.*

It is far too easy to allow circumstances to cripple us. And when they do, we can choose to accept them as insurmountable and hobble on emotional crutches. Or we can look them squarely in the face and declare, as Pitt did, *I walk upon impossibilities!*

_____

by Susan Shimkovitz

Grace Lessons from a Puppy

Oliver, my Italian Greyhound, is five months old. Like a child, he's attached to my hip.

He may socialize with others, but at the end of the day he wants to sit on my lap or lie next to me. When I get home, he jumps on me like he hasn't seen me in ages. When we go for a car ride, he wants to sit on my lap. If he's cold, he wants to be wrapped up in my hoodie (while I'm still wearing it).

And while all of this is cute, there are times when he's not cute at all. Like when he poops in the house, or jumps on my piano and walks across the keys, or chews up a roll of toilet paper, or rips up the blinds, or eats my hair, or drinks out of the toilet.

He knows when he's done wrong because he tries to distract me from seeing the crime scene. And when he does get caught, he quickly covers his face with his front paws. And you guessed it, no matter how angry I am, I can't help but laugh at his guilty reaction.

With champion bloodlines on both sides, Oliver should be quick at learning tricks and commands. But he's not exactly the sharpest crayon in the box and has a long ways to go.

I cannot tell you how many times I have threatened to sell Oliver to the circus or send him back to Arkansas. But at the end of the day, I decide he's worth the pain and frustration he causes now and then.

I think that's how God's grace works too. Time and time again I mess up, I fall short, I destroy things I have no business touching. Yet God gives me a second, a third, a fourth—and 749 chances and more.

No matter how big my mess, God's always there to clean up after me. *It's okay,* He says, *You're still learning and you've got a long ways to go. I love you too much to give up on you.*

by Heather Joy Vires

A Lei of Protection

Nepal's culture and history are drenched with folklore and festivals. For every event, there's a story. One of my favorites is the story behind Bhai Tika (Brother's Day).

King Bali Hang was very ill. His sister, Jamuna, watched over him day and night, praying he would be well again. But he only got worse. One day Yamaraj, the God of Death, came knocking to claim the soul of King Bali Hang. Jamuna pled and bargained for her brother's soul, but Yamaraj would not budge.

Finally she begged for just a little more time with her brother. She had just completed the traditional Bhai Tika puja to honor her brother: smeared his forehead with a red tikka, sprinkled his face with water and adorned his neck with a garland of the round bright magenta flowers, Supadi Phool. She tearfully told Yamaraj he could have her brother after three things happened: the tikka faded, the water dried and the flowers wilted.

It seemed like a fair deal to Yamaraj. So he waited. Soon enough, the tikka faded and the water dried. But the flowers would not wilt. Tired of waiting, he left. Over the next year, every now and then Yamaraj sent someone to check on the Supadi Phool. The flowers simply refused to wilt.

When the next Bhai Tika rolled around, Yamaraj came knocking again. But this time, it was to honor Jamuna's love for her brother and to grant King Bali Hang a very long and healthy life.

Bhai Tika continues to be a major festival today with plenty of color and flamboyance. Sisters present brothers with fruit, gifts and a lei of flowers that represent their prayers of protection and a long life for their brothers.

Today, do something special for your brother or your sister—or the person who is like one to you.

* Globe Amaranth in English. Some say that the flower had soft petals just like most other flowers until it fell under the spell of Jamuna's love for her brother.

---

by Fylvia Fowler Kline

Finding my Voice Again

It was the first day of school, and Dennis, the drama teacher and I were chatting. I asked about his plans for the fall musical. He beamed and said, *I want to do the Sound of Music. I'm going to include alumni and faculty in the cast. I want you to be Mother Abbess.*

I was flattered, but surprised. The role of Mother Abbess? She sings the signature piece, *Climb Every Mountain.* I had not sung seriously in more than 30 years. Stultifying stage fright tightened my throat. I withered inside; I knew I couldn't do it.

Singing used to be my first love. In college I sang constantly—in the car, in the shower, between classes. It gave me such joy. I even sang with friends in coffee houses, dorm lounges and choirs. My voice had once defined me. But I hadn't used it in many years.

I said no. But Dennis insisted, *You'll be great. It would be awesome for the school and the kids to have you on stage. Have faith. You can do this.*

Dennis was counting on me. Soon, so was the rest of the school. And something I'd heard somewhere echoed in my heart: *Faith does.*

So I found a quiet spot and began—tried—to sing. I quickly found out what heartbreak sounds like! My once lyrical voice was now buried under years and layers of wife, mommy and teacher. I sounded tired, old and desperate.

I cried nearly every time I rehearsed—not from the strain of practice, but for the loss of the gift that had once brought me such joy. But I kept working. They were counting on me.

I listened to the lyrics: *Climb every mountain, follow every rainbow, till you find your dream.* I began to see the song as a prayer and I began to have faith in myself for the first time in my life.

I had to believe that I could do this. Through doubt and pain, I kept rehearsing.

Opening night. End of Act I. It was all up to me. I flung my prayer heavenward. And it returned to me a million-fold.

I heard the Spirit whispering, *I knew it all along.* Yes, *faith does.*

---

by Tess Wigginton

Angels in Disguise

Then, in your desperate condition, you called out to God. He got you out in the nick of time. Psalm 107:6

Thirty teens and two adults were at a church camping event in the Joshua Tree National Forest. It was late Saturday afternoon and almost time to start fixing dinner. But the kids wanted to climb, one last time, the rock cliff that towered about a hundred feet over the camp site.

The older teens who functioned as counselors were put in charge of the group heading out for the last climb. Reminding everyone to stay together and to stay close enough to hear the public address system, the group was sent off while the two adults began fixing supper.

When supper was ready, the leader used the public address system to call the hikers back to camp. Time went by, the sun was setting and there were no signs of them. Those in camp began searching everywhere. Nothing. They gathered together and prayed. Still nothing.

Expecting to return early, the group had not taken any flashlights. After what seemed like eternity, one of the counselors returned with news: The group was stuck at a precarious point of the cliff that was difficult to get to and near impossible to get off.

Immediately the two adult leaders left with flashlights. To get to the group, they had to jump over several drop-offs of about 80 feet that spanned about 6 feet apart. Once they reached the group, they realized they needed to find another way down. Huddling everyone together, they prayed, *God you know our situation, you see the dangers around us. Please help us.* Just as they said *Amen,* two men showed up saying they had been on these rocks all day and knew an easy way down.

The two men, who had flashlights, took the lead and the rest followed closely. The men were right; the path down was safe and manageable. During the entire trek back down, the group followed the two strangers, keeping a close eye on them and their flashlights.

But when they finally reached the valley floor, the two men were nowhere to be found. They were gone as quickly as they appeared. Everyone looked around—but saw no other flashlight, heard no sound of feet walking away. There was no sight of the men.

Truly God sends his angels to encamp around those that fear Him and He delivers them.

_____

by Doina Jeffery

The Secret in the Elevator

I held the elevator door open as she stepped in, deftly balancing her crutches and packages.

It was a slow ride to the next floor. Energetic, outgoing and young, I attempted to make small talk. When we got to her floor, I began to help her with her packages. And that's when it happened: She turned around and gave me the tongue lashing of my life. Firm and venomous, she told me to mind my own business and stay out of her stuff.

Embarrassed, hurt and very angry, I couldn't understand why my efforts to be a good citizen were received with such disdain. Working with her in the same building did not make it any easier.

I began to avoid her and also began praying that the Lord would resolve this for me in His own time.

I moved on to other jobs and the elevator incident and the woman were forgotten.

Some 15 years later, in another elevator, guess who walked in! I smiled at her, realizing God had not forgotten. That second smile 15 years later has evolved into a friendship. We sometimes share rides home, we giggle at the water fountain.

One day she said, *I know you from somewhere before.*

I responded, *We used to work in the same office many years ago.* I didn't see the point of helping her remember any more.

Had I held on to resentment, I would have lost the opportunity for a new friend 15 years down the road.

What happened then in the elevator is a secret I share with my Father who knows what it takes to mold me into what I am today.

_____

by Joy Alexander

The Coat

As summer gives way to fall in Oregon, the wind picks up and ushers in the cold and rain and misery that are the prelude to winter.

On one of those windy days, I noticed a young man without a coat. He stood there shivering. I couldn't help but ask, *Where's your coat?*

He smiled sheepishly, looked down and somewhat embarrassedly said he didn't have a coat. I didn't say anything more. But every now and then, I'd see him again—cold and without a coat. We talked once in a while, and I soon learned that he had just gotten married and that between the two of them they had four kids and one meager job.

It was about three weeks to Christmas and I was badgered by thoughts of the young man and his family. Giving in to my instincts, I prayed about the situation and talked to my husband about it. We both agreed that I must get the man a coat.

While talking to him the next day, I learned that he and his wife were going to take the kids to see Santa in the mall. I said I'd meet them there. When I met him at the mall, I told him that the Lord had directed me to buy him a coat and he could not refuse the gift. He graciously accepted my offer.

As we headed towards the store, I noticed how very tall he was and prayed I'd have enough money to purchase a coat in his irregular size. To my surprise the coat that fit him perfectly was marked down 60 percent; at the register, another $35 was taken off the price!

Amazed at how little the coat cost me and that I still had money leftover, I looked over and noticed how old and worn the wife's coat was. You guessed it—the leftover money was just enough to buy her a coat too.

When the Lord asks you to do good, He blesses you and your resources. What a day that was! I believe I received the bigger blessing that day.

_____

by Laurie Owen

Thatha Taught Me

On the shores of the Arabian Sea, the little village sits, tucked at India's side. To the north of the common well live the fishermen, to the south the weavers. Thatha* lived on the south side, on Weavers' Street. Neither a fisherman nor a weaver, he technically didn't belong. But He lived there for more than 40 years, until he died at the age of 82.

An effective pastor with a church in town, he lived a hot, dusty hour-long bus ride away in this village, without the luxury of plumbing and electricity. He chose to live there for no other reason but because he felt called to share Jesus in that village.

Every morning Thatha would wake up at five o'clock, open his windows and sing out of tune. He sang of hope, of God's love, of Jesus' soon coming. And then he'd kneel by the open window and pray aloud for the drunken neighbor who beat his wife the night before, for the money lender who charged an exorbitant interest rate to the young widow, for the boy trying to get through high school, for the fishermen who had a bad night at sea. All day long, he would help, share, counsel. He chose to reflect Jesus not just in his village but also in the surrounding villages. Thatha even built a chapel that shared a wall with his home.

He held prayer meetings and church services there with the doors wide open. Sometimes he'd have a visitor or two. Most often, there were none.

All he had to show for 40 years of exemplary Christian living in that village was one baptism. That too, not in his village, but in another far away. Yet, he was content.

At the end of his life, Thatha lay in bed by the open window. Outside stood fishermen and weavers—two, three and four generations of them. They came to say goodbye to the man they loved.

Even today, they speak of the man who prayed, encouraged and loved. And in the other village, where the lone man was baptized, are many, many more Christians. Sometimes I wish Thatha had lived to see his faith germinate. But the fact that he didn't says so much more. His life was like a spring that gives and gives of itself, enriching some, quenching the thirst of others. A spring that doesn't dry up just to measure how much it is needed.

From Thatha I've learnt not to ask why, not to tally my little victories. I've learnt that I don't need to see the difference I make. It is not my glory but His.

*Grandpa

---

by Fylvia Fowler Kline

Empty to be Filled

Spending quiet time in prayer and meditation on the Word of God is an important part of our daily routine. However, it's not always easy to fill our hearts and minds with the Word when we have already filled them with the things of the world. Our minds are often packed with lists that need to be done, people we need to contact. So much is crammed into our day that we need to first empty our hearts and minds before the Lord can fill us up.

Jesus did this throughout his time on earth. *While it was still night, way before dawn, he got up and went out to a secluded spot and prayed (Mark 1:35).* Sometimes he went out farther in the mountains to find a spot to pray (Mark 6:46). A lonely place (Luke 5:16) or a peaceful garden (Mark 14:32-34) was where Jesus went to get away from the noise of life and to fill Himself with the presence of God.

Jesus recognized the need to empty Himself and be refilled with the Father every day. More importantly, He consistently kept that time of renewal sacred and safe.

This week, look for opportunities to empty yourself of all that weighs you down. Find a spot outside and watch the sunset. Fall asleep under a canopy of stars. Go for a walk by yourself. Then make that experience your secret haven—a place to be emptied of self and be filled by the Spirit.

by Amanda Johnson

Caught in a Marital Storm

It begins with a long list of things to get done. And I'm growing tired and feeling stressed. I may not do anything wrong per se, but all the right ingredients are present to form a cloud on the horizon.

My husband enters the picture. He notices my stressed attitude, my preoccupation with busyness, and feels overlooked, maybe even ignored. He makes a casual comment to bring this fact to my attention. All of sudden, I feel guilty, frustrated and burdened even more. That's when the cloud begins to build and pick up strength.

I have a choice at this point. I can realize what's developing or I can keep my nose to the grindstone and snap back at him. Very often, I am not self-aware enough to take this check-in perspective and I've, most likely, neglected my time with God as well. So not only do I operate with just my own strength, but I also miss out on the clarity and grace that God can bring to my heart. That's when lightning begins to negatively charge my marriage.

Before my husband and I know it, the storm gains momentum. We go in circles arguing and being defensive, giving birth to the proverbial vicious cycle. You might say that a tornado begins to spiral.

You'd think at this point, we'd take cover— *hide under the wings of the Almighty.* But no, we are like fearless, stupid storm watchers who like the thrill of watching the fury of our relationship swirl around in the winds of our pride and fear.

When all is said and done, we wake up to the devastation that only a real tornado can bring. There's damage to our marriage and we've drifted apart. We've allowed our anger and confusion to rule the day and ruin our union.

But there is hope when we serve a God who is able to speak and command the storm to stop. In ourselves, we don't have the power, but in His compassion, grace, mercy and love, we find the ingredients to calm the storm.

---

by Beth Steffanaik

Preparation

So stay awake, alert. You have no idea what day your Master will show up. Matthew 24:42

Over the course of those few days, people went about their business-as-usual ways, unaware of and unprepared for anything out of the ordinary. No one—not even the smiling weatherman who predicted an average day—knew there was a winter storm brewing just over the horizon.

So when the city awoke to eight inches of snow the next morning, everyone and everything became paralyzed. The city was in a panic.

As I settled in for an unexpected day of rest, I thought how this storm had taken everyone by surprise. But I also remembered my daddy's words to me growing up in Michigan. *Ruth-Ann,* he would say, *Always be prepared. Never allow your gas tank to get less than half full. Keep extra blankets, rock salt, a shovel and chains in the trunk of your car. Make sure your cupboards are always stocked with food. And never forget that it's wintertime.*

I could also hear my Heavenly Father's Word clearly speaking, *But the exact day and hour? No one knows that, not even heaven's angels, not even the Son.*

Only the Father knows (Matthew 24:36). It's preparation time. Never allow your lamp to get empty of the Holy Spirit's oil; stock up on the manna, God's Word, for nourishment; reserve extra time with God; and always be ready to tell someone about His soon return.

_____

by Ruth-Ann Thompson

Some Kind of Mother's Love

I am good at burying memories of my not-so-proud moments. I'm really, really good at it. But then sometimes, something random and innocuous trips my memory blocker and I remember a moment—in detailed clarity and with all the original embarrassment.

Today a cute little dog named Tia was what made me remember one of those moments.

It was about the third week of our life in Nepal. We were still the fresh, drenched-behind-the-ears missionaries getting used to many things—a stone and marble home without heat in the Himalayan winter; scrawny chickens that looked like turtle doves at the dinner table; boiling and filtering water to drink; showing some respect to the soldiers carrying machine guns along the highway; topping off a sandwich with Yak cheese instead of Swiss.

Life was exciting and adventuresome. Even in that which we didn't care for, we reveled in the experience (like the first time we realized the delicious treat was deep fried buffalo innards). Even when listening to warnings from the US Embassy officials about living in Maoist territory, we felt a Superman-like wave of the thrill of danger. I was like Super Mom, Super Wife and Super Missionary molded into one tough, good-looking woman. At least that's how I saw myself—until one dark, so-quiet-you-can-hear-the-silence night.

It must have been about two in the morning. I was fast asleep. So were Roy, the kids and the dog. Then all of a sudden, out of the stillness, came the loudest thunderous sound I had ever heard. In that instant between sleep and wakefulness, I knew it was a bomb.

Screaming, I jumped out of bed and began running down the hallway towards the front door. Alongside me our dog, Wrinkles, was also running, trying to beat me to the door. I was out the door and in the middle of the open yard before I realized that I had run out of the house without thinking of Roy or the kids. I was just thinking of getting myself out to safety. Looking through the open front door, I saw my family looking at me like I was crazy.

Some Superwoman I turned out to be. The fact that Wrinkles was far from being man's best friend that night by trying to get out before saving her family didn't make me feel any better either.

---

by Fylvia Fowler Kline

I've Been Robbed

Surfing the Internet one day, I found an interesting article about the piracy of eBooks. It made me a bit nervous. So I did some more poking around and discovered that my book had been downloaded over 400,000 times from certain sites.

It made me mad. I felt like 400,000 copies of my book were stolen from me. What was worse is that I couldn't get credit for the book having reached all those people.

I went back to those sites the next morning. But by then, they were now non-existent.

I could have sat there and rung my hands together, crying out to God to protect my books. And I don't think it would have been a terrible choice. We're a single income family that has struggles just like anyone else. For crying out loud, I make my own laundry soap and cleaning supplies to help save money. I cook from scratch and shop at bargain shops to save even more.

My book being distributed without me getting credit or money is unfair, especially since I've worked so hard.

So this is what I choose to do. I choose to pray that

- the stolen books touch hearts for Christ.
- God uses me and my books for His honor and glory.
- I have the right heart attitude.
- I continue to write for Him.

By choosing to let God use the piracy of my books, I've just become a missionary without leaving my home. Since every book I've written focuses on the plan of salvation, I am going to claim God's promise that His Word won't return void.

I don't do this because I'm perfect. Um, absolutely not! I get angry. I get frustrated. I get downright evil at times. I'm. Not. Perfect.

But I also know I've been forgiven.

And so I choose to forgive those who have wronged me because the King of kings forgives this pitiful, wretched sinner—over and over again.

---

by Amanda Stephan

Bitter Water

Consider it a sheer gift, friends, when tests and challenges come at you from all sides. You know that under pressure, your faith-life is forced into the open and shows its true colors. So don't try to get out of anything prematurely. Let it do its work so you become mature and well-developed, not deficient in any way. James 1:2-4

The Israelites had been traveling days without fresh water. They were dehydrated *(Exodus 15:22-17).*

Picture the Israelites—the entire multitude of them— suffering from the symptoms of dehydration at the same time. Weakness, extreme thirst, irregular weak heartbeat, an inability to think clearly. Can you imagine more than two million people suffering from these symptoms together? Now imagine the reaction of this large group when they saw water for the first time in days!

I see a rush of men, women, children—both old and young—stampeding over one another—in a race toward water, toward relief from their suffering. But when they took that first gulp of water, they spewed it out in disgust. A seemingly cruel joke from heaven, the water was bitter!

Let's go back to the story of the bitter water of Marah. Notice how the story ends. God doesn't lead them to new waters. Instead, he reaches down to heal, to sweeten, the bitter water. In healing the bitter water, God wrought joy from their disappointment. Think about this for a moment. Perhaps their difficulty or anguish is what made their joy all the more sweeter, their relief all the greater. While it is difficult to grasp the idea of experiencing troubles for great joy, this story tells us that God can indeed sweeten our bitter water.

In Exodus 15:25, God reminds His people that He is the God who heals. God will heal the bitterness and give you rest. Do you need God to sweeten the bitter water of pain and disappointment? Then trust in His healing.

---

by Sharon Claassen

Autumn's Love

I will talk to the Father, and he'll provide you another Friend so that you will always have someone with you. John 14:16

I see God's love through the spectacular autumn colors bursting and shouting out, *God loves me.* The Sunkist orange, flaming red, and vibrant yellow leaves are glowing colors that speak of endurance .

There are three radiant, blazing red trees standing together in front of me. They remind me of God the Father, the Son and the Holy Spirit. Their brilliant stature reminds me of their ceaseless and continuous love for me.

On your feet now—applaud God! Bring a gift of laughter, sing yourselves into his presence. Know this: God is God, and God, God. He made us; we didn't make him. We're his people, his well-tended sheep (Psalm 100:1-3).

As the Holy Spirit burns within my heart, soul and mind, He brands me as His and proclaims to the entire universe, *I passionately love Mary! I live within her and will set up home in her heart forever.*

This is the promise of the indwelling Christ which shouts with each vibrant autumn leaf. God's love prints are on every spectacular leaf.

May the same love be stamped on your heart, soul and mind. And may your life display the brilliant multi-colored representation of Him as seen in the shimmering colors of nature.

_____

by Mary Maxson

Family Chronicles

Who am I, my Master God, and what is my family, that you have brought me to this place in life? 1 Chronicles 17:16

Suppose you were to lose everything you held dear? What would you cling to if all that had once been tangible in your life were no more?

The Israelites often found themselves in a similar situation. Their history is filled with much disappointment and discouragement. Their story alternates episodes of hope with those of despair. The book of Chronicles finds them at the end of half a century of captivity. During this time they lost more than their freedom; they lost their sense of identity. At such a milestone, the book of Chronicles urges them to remember their glorious past, to recollect the best of times. The narrative is an effort to help the Israelites get in touch with who they were in God's plan.

Do you see the similarities between the Israelites and us? Are we at a time in our lives when we need to remember our glorious past? Like the Israelites, we too are a race of hope. Although our past has its interludes of disheartenment, we have many stories that beget hope in our present. Forgetting where the Lord has led us will only jeopardize our future. Maybe it's a good idea to chronicle our miracles, struggles and joyous events. And periodically, re-read the stories at family gatherings to strengthen our hope in Christ, to see where we fit into God's divine plan.

---

by Fylvia Fowler Kline

The Kindest Gift

I am a strong person. I have weathered broken relationships, the ebb and flow of friends and finances, health problems and the death of beloved pets. Even with all that, I was woefully unprepared for my father's death the day after Christmas.

It was a long weekend of sleepless nights in the cardiac care unit, coupled with the inherent drama of the family dynamic as my mother, sister and I jockeyed for primacy. After Dad's quiet passing Monday morning and the surreal discussions and decisions that occur after a death, my husband and I, exhausted and numb, drove 200 miles to the sanctuary of our home, far far away from the sadness, the anger, the drama.

I had responsibilities at home to distract me from the terrible reality of the loss. At work, there were more distractions: Payroll to be submitted. Deposits to be made. Paper to be shuffled. And I, the stoic, dry-eyed, responsible daughter who always found comfort and solace in work, went into the office to do those tasks that could be accomplished quickly.

I went in Tuesday. The Day After.

My colleagues are an amazing group of women—strong, self-reliant, creative and funny, without behaving like characters in an Oprah book club selection. Their individual quirks are part of their charm and their success.

One in particular I really admire. A thoughtful, intuitive writer and a deeply spiritual woman, she has a wonderfully wry sense of humor that always makes me laugh. Close to my age and with challenges in her past that she has overcome but that haven't defined her, we speak a common language and at times I marvel at my good fortune to have met such a calm, wise woman. Her particular quirk is that she is not a hugger. She resists the efforts of all to embrace her for no other reason than she just doesn't care for it. We affectionately make a closed circle with our arms for her when the occasion warrants a hug. It's nothing personal; hugging is just not her thing. She finds it more comfortable to express her joy or concern in a beautifully crafted message or a kind supportive word.

When I went into the office that Tuesday, The Day After, this wonderfully kind friend came around a corner, looked me in the eye, and without a word or hesitation, enveloped me in a hug. And then I finally really cried for my dad.

And that is kindest gift anyone has given me.

---

by Cathy Watt

By the Waters

There's nothing more soothing than the burbling sound of water rushing over silt and rock, accompanied by the background noises of blue jays and crickets and the smell of wild grass. There's something about the sounds of nature that envelope you in a cocoon of protection from the troubles and cares of the world.

But you don't have to be in the middle of the country to find your gurgling-brook moments. Even in the midst of a concrete jungle, nature finds a way. It may be a favorite park; a patch of grass used as a dog run by your apartment building; or the butterfly you find perched on the windshield of your parked car. Nature is in the very air we breathe, and wherever there is nature, you have the most visible evidence of God. A deep, full breath of afternoon air can be the kind of break that reminds you of a *peace that transcends understanding.*

Visualization is also a powerful gift that God has given you. Just close your eyes in a quiet room and allow yourself to see, feel, hear and smell the perfect brook. See yourself lying in the tall grass, your eyes closed, your breathing even and deep. Block out your worries, your responsibilities, your needs and even your failings. Then reach for that inner part of yourself where you can best hear the still small voice of the Holy Spirit.

You don't have to travel hundreds of miles and spend a lot of money for vacation. Try having your own mini-vacation every day. Envision your brook, meditate on God and listen to your inner voice today. The closer that voice is to the will of God, the happier you will be.

_____

by Ramona Levacy

Angels in Cowboy Boots

Every time I'm in trouble I call on you, confident that you'll answer.
Psalm 86:7

It was not the first time fear and frustration had me praying for wisdom on my firstborn son's behalf. Since Joseph's birth, his life has been peppered with difficulties—fears of carcinoma, respiratory problems, and then at just 20 months, a misdiagnosed fever led to a discovery of petit mal seizures. This led to some neurological damage by the time he was six years old.

Even though he continues with physical and mental challenges, I am glad God healed him from seizures when he was 11.

With each set of circumstances and challenges, the Lord makes a way. When I feel helpless at the end of pursuing what often appears to be a dead end, the Lord opens a way where there had been none.

The most recent was a bullying situation. The two-headed monster of fear and frustration reared its ugly head once more with the report of knife threats. Although we knew we could intervene, my husband and I realized Joseph would have to face this very real fear for himself. We prayed with him and sent him to school believing God would place his angels around him and protect him. We gave our own fears to God and prayed throughout the day.

The story Joseph told us that afternoon brought us to tears, thankfulness and laughter. There had indeed been another incident at lunch. But this time, he did not have to face his intimidator by himself. A boy Joseph had befriended and some others stood up in my son's defense and diffused the threats. They were a group of kickers or cowboys.

Joseph, I said through the tears, *I knew the Lord would surround you with angels, but I didn't know they would be wearing cowboy boots!*

---

by Sharon Patterson

Small Degrees of Change

August 2008 brought to New York City heat waves and concerns about the rise in utility costs. That was when the United Nations' secretariat building decided to take the lead in energy conservation. Employees were asked to wear light clothing, the thermostat was turned up five degrees to 77 F everywhere except the conference room, where it was set at 75 F.

The result was worth the small change: In August alone, the UN reduced their utility bill by $100,000! Plus they saved 4,400 million pounds of steam—which is the same as saving several hundred tons of carbon dioxide. It was estimated that if they turned down the thermostat in the winter months, the savings would be about a million dollars a year!

Often we underestimate the difference little changes and compromises make in our community, homes and relationships. Whether adjusting the thermostat by a couple of degrees or quitting that little habit that irritates a loved one, that one change could be what it takes to make life a little more meaningful.

---

by Fylvia Fowler Kline

Windy

Today I saw a very strange occurrence—a man with a leaf blower cleaning the debris off the sidewalk and parking lot on a very windy day. The word futile comes to mind.

It's like handing the cars keys to 16-year-olds and telling them to drive carefully. You know the minute they get around the corner, there will be tires squealing and loud music thumping through the speakers.

It makes me think about the story of Esther in the Bible. What was the reason for that book in the Bible? Don't get me wrong, it was the first book of the Bible I read all the way through. It's a story any girl would love. It's terribly tragic in the beginning, but ends in triumph. It has a loving uncle, a beauty pageant, several dazzling banquets, and intrigue woven throughout the plot line. But not many would see it as the perfect Bible study material.

After completing an in-depth study on the Book of Esther in my Bible study class, our teacher asked the question, *Why do you think this book is in our Bibles?* Some scholars believe the story of Esther is a made-up fairy tale because there is no reference to God anywhere in the book.

As I sat listening to people justify the existence of Esther in the Bible, I thoughtfully reviewed the story. And all of a sudden it hit me—Philemon! It's the one-chapter book in the New Testament where Paul is begging forgiveness on behalf of a servant, and . . . oops, that's a bit of a spoiler alert. If you haven't read Philemon, spend the 5 minutes and do it now. I'll wait :)

Did you see it? There it is, right in front of you. It's the story of salvation. On behalf of us sinners, Jesus gave His life. On behalf of her people, Esther petitioned the king. On behalf of his servant Onesimus, Paul petitioned his friend Philemon. In all three of these stories, the theme is salvation.

When referring to Onesimus, Paul calls him *son* and *my heart (verses 10 and 12, NIV)*. As my mother says of the book of Philemon, *If this were the only book in the Bible, we would still have the story of salvation.* And I think the same is true of the story of Esther. If it were the only book in the Bible, we would still have that wonderful story of salvation.

---

by Cynthia Ward

The Ebb and Flow

The beautiful coastline is bright and inviting. Hammock-filled trees offer unobstructed views of clear blue waters splashing at the white sandy beach. Each wave brings refreshing coolness. Warm water, clear blue skies, and peaceful rest offer reprieve from storms past.

But circumstances change quickly and with full force from the ocean's tide, each wave erodes the sands of hope, peace, and strength. With each pull of the tide, joy ebbs away. Salty spray spits wet, cold, saturating concerns from the mighty sea; white caps topple each attempt to stand. No plan, no will to fight, no calm is afforded in its wake. Lungs fill with spume. Confidence is coughed out; foamy doubt inhaled. Despair's thick fog sets in; all visibility is gone.

Such is the ebb and flow of life. Good and bad, up and down, weariness and rest, faith and doubt. I've navigated these waters long enough to know there is constant change and what is here today may be washed out with the morning's tide. Bright azure skies turn grey in an instant. Clear waters suddenly fill with entangling weeds. Warm rays give way to soaking rain. That which is seemingly predictable is erratic and uncontrollable.

The Bible reminds us in Ecclesiastes 3 that life is filled with seasons. Such a contradiction, this constant change; yet it is the very foundation of our days. We hold no power over the laws of existence. The rules of nature prevail whether we like them or not. And while it is sometimes difficult to sail across stormy deeps, we can cross with the confidence that God is the constant in our times of change. Even if He doesn't alter the course of our ships or speak calm into our seas, He declares peace over us. In the midst of the reeling, overwhelming tempest He whispers in tranquil tone, *Be still and know that I am God (Psalm 46:10).*

by Deidra Manning

The Pain of Hurting

Ever had something feel solid and right, but then, unexpectedly, from nowhere, everything falls apart? The pain can be so deep that nothing can ease it or take it away. The tearing in our heart renders us completely numb.

Even when you are a bystander and the pain isn't yours, it's difficult to simply stand and watch someone else's pain take its course. All you want to do is jump in and take away the hurt.

Reassure yourself. Start by saying, *No, you have not been stupid!* Give it time: cry, rant and pray for relief from the gut-wrenching anguish.

Be kind to yourself. You won't feel like eating, talking, making decisions, cleaning! It takes too much energy to even try to think! Curl up in a ball and bawl, if that's what you feel like doing! A little pity-party is okay.

Take a bath! Take a walk! Get out of the four walls that have become an enclosure and fill your lungs with fresh air. Watch people getting on with their lives, although that'll feel surreal. Since your hurt is so intense you will probably expect others to know about know how you feel. But the reality is that they don't and won't!

But God is always there and always understands how you feel. Lean on Him for all you are worth and you'll be given strength and comfort beyond your understanding.

If your heart is broken, you'll find God right there; if you're kicked in the gut, he'll help you catch your breath (Psalm 34:18). He heals the heartbroken and bandages their wounds (Psalm 147:3).

_____

by Patricia Day

My Tiffany

I spent part of that Sunday antiquing with Roy, searching for an end table. As we went up and down the aisles, I'd see something I liked and let out a *wow* or an *ooh* to express my delight. The more impressive the antique, the louder my *wow's* and *ooh's* were.

When I saw the Tiffany lamp, my *WOW* was so loud it startled the quiet, elderly couple with whom we shared the aisle. The perfect shades of browns and greens with hints of the palest blue were just right for my living room. But since we were there for an end table and not a lamp, I pulled myself together and moved on. Two hours and two pairs of sore feet later, we hadn't found the perfect end table. So we left without a purchase, but feeling good about having spent some quality time together.

The rest of the day was the usual kind of Sunday, filled with chores around the house. I spent most of that afternoon buried in boxes and cobwebs in the garage till it was time to fix dinner. Everything was the usual until I went back in the house to find the Tiffany lamp sitting pretty in my living room!

A gift given for no particular reason except to say, *You are special to me* is the best kind of gift.

This week surprise someone with something to make them feel special. Better yet, set aside one day a month for a random act of thoughtfulness.

---

by Fylvia Fowler Kline

Jesus Hates Spam

I hate spam. Period.

No, I don't care to know how you earned $5000 in three days. No, little Russian girl, I don't want to be your friend. No, I'm not looking for a pair of knock-off Nike shoes. No, I don't want your highly-intellectual advice about how to better my website.

I had just spent more time than I had to clean out the spam on my blog. And I was annoyed.

I wonder if that's how Jesus feels when he looks at Christians. I wonder if He hates Christian spam—the kind that twist biblical truth into pointless rules and shoots them off into the Christian community just to condemn anyone who doesn't follow said rules. That's not cool; it's annoying.

To all that Christian spam, I say this with the power of God's redeeming grace:

No, I don't want your legalistic rules being slapped on my life. No, I don't care about the hypocritical judgments in your every glare and tone of voice. No, I'm not interested in your knock-off brand of spirituality. No, Pharisee, I'm not the least bit interested in following your example.

So save your spammy Christianity for someone else and leave me alone to live my life the way Jesus has told me to.

And God, give me the clarity of your vision to see the best in everyone.

Reexamine your attitudes towards others. Are any of them spammy? Make a decision today to be more genuine and less judgmental.

---

by Heather Joy Vires

Where are You?

*The Man and his Wife hid in the trees of the garden, hid
from God. God called to the Man: "Where are you?" Genesis 3:8, 9*

Contemplating on these verses, I wondered how this
scenario would play out in my life. *Where and when
would God look for me? And what is the garden that
God expects me to tend?*

When we began planning our yard, we used
landscaping books and sketched out individual
portions that came together as one big unified
garden. I applied the same principle to life and saw
how there are different sections. From home and
family, to church and ministries, to work and play, I
come in contact with many in my life garden.

No part of my garden is exclusively mine. It all
belongs to God; I am merely the caretaker. When I
look at my life as God's garden, I have a fresh new
perspective of the mundane. Whether I'm at work,
being a mother or just pulling weeds, the moment
holds a tremendous opportunity to represent God to
anyone who may be around.

_____

by Glenda Maxson-Davidson

Through a Dare

You will experience for yourselves the truth, and the truth will free you.
John 8:32

The devil would say, *Jump.* And I'd respond, *How far?*
That was my life. One jump after another. There was
an emptiness in me that nothing seemed to fill. Not
my jumps, not my work, not even God.

Growing up, we attended different churches. After a
few Sundays at one, mom and dad would argue.
Jealousy over the pastor talking to mom or an older
woman talking to dad was usually the cause. And
again we'd start going to another church.

While training to be a nurse, it was easy to deny
God's presence. I reasoned that if there were a God,
people wouldn't suffer and die. My job after
graduation at a coronary intensive care unit only
proved even more that there was no God.

My life continued to be reckless and empty. But there
was one thing that gave me joy—my bright orange
1972 Heavy Chevy Chevelle. I invested a good chunk
of my time and resources to keep it looking good. I
even had my own parking space at the hospital.

So you can imagine how I felt when another Heavy Chevy was parked in my space one day! Searching the hospital, I found the culprit—a young medic from the army base close by who was working his off-hours as an orderly. Confronting him, I gave him a piece of my mind. He didn't say anything and just looked at me like I was crazy! He never parked in my space again.

A few months later, I ran into him again. He was in a hurry, explaining to his co-worker, *I need to hurry back to base and change for church.* What a great opportunity I had to ridicule him.

Speaking loud enough for everyone to hear, I said, *What a weirdo! BORING! Can't you find anything better to do?*

This time he did respond. He dared me to go to church with him. And not being one to turn down a dare, I went.

And something happened the moment I walked into that church. Not only did I feel something fill the emptiness within me; but I also felt the warmth of the friendly people around me.

Right there I knew I had been looking in all the wrong places. This was it. This church. This community. This God. And all it took was a dare .

---

by Vicky Tibbetts

Measuring Life with Chips

My first few weeks of missionary life in Nepal were awful. I felt trapped, imprisoned and deprived of necessities—like heat in my home, television sitcoms, hot showers, high speed Internet and people who used deodorant.

But most of all, I was outraged that there was neither potato chips nor cheesecake. Unable to imagine six years without potato chips and cheesecake, I was an extremely grumpy servant of the Lord.

And then one frigidly cold Friday night, wearing three pairs of woolen socks and wrapped in a thick blanket, I read about Polycarp. A disciple of Apostle John, he was arrested when the Roman Emperor, Marcus Aurelius, was persecuting Christians. During the trial, Polycarp was told that the only way to get his freedom was to give up Christ. In response, Polycarp said, *Eighty-six years have I served Him, and He never did me any injury; how then can I blaspheme my King and my Savior?*

Polycarp's allegiance to his Lord cost him his life. He was bound like a sacrificial lamb and set on fire. While the flames rose around him, Polycarp looked up into the heavens and said, *I give You thanks that You have counted me worthy of this day and this hour.*

Polycarp made me look and feel like a selfish, whiny crybaby. I gave myself a good mental spanking and vowed to make the most of my six years. The result? I'd go back for another six years if I had a chance!

And I'll always remember that by our second year there Lay's potato chips AND Philadelphia cream cheese made their debut in Nepal!

_____

by Fylvia Fowler Kline

The Staff

Your trusty shepherd's crook makes me feel secure. Psalm 23:4

When my husband goes walking by the pond, he always grabs one of his walking sticks. It makes him look like a mountain man—rugged, strong, surefooted, the outdoorsy kind of guy. My mountain man of a husband has always taken care of me and loved me through thick and thin, the good, the bad and the ugly. Just like my Lord and Savior.

We're his people, his well-tended sheep (Psalm 100:3). Jesus is the great shepherd who goes ahead of me and points the way, showing me lessons I might not have learned if I did not follow Him and His staff.

The shepherd's rod protects the sheep from other animals. My Lord's staff is something to lean on, to trust. Even when the path is rocky with potholes here and there, He will lead me to the pond.

If I follow my Savior's leading, I know I'll be fine at the end of my journey. He doesn't promise a smooth path through life, but He does promise to be with me through every happening. He is either ahead of me, leading me where I should go; or by my side assuring me of His presence; or He carries me when I feel I can't go on any more.

Although pretty close to perfect, my husband is not perfect. Yet I can't help but smile when I see him walking in front of me, his staff in hand.

Thank you Lord, for being my Great Shepherd and for giving me an earthly one as well.

_____

by Kristin Bridgman

When Plans Unravel

I know what I'm doing. I have it all planned out—plans to take care of you, not abandon you, plans to give you the future you hope for. Jeremiah 29:11

I like knowing what to expect. I like maps, itineraries, schedules. I can't sit down in church without first grabbing a program bulletin. It's comforting to be informed.

So when I was surprised by the discovery that I was pregnant, I dashed to the nearest bookstore to purchase *What to Expect When You're Expecting.* Of course, even the book couldn't answer all my questions, the biggest and most selfish of which was, *Is this going to completely ruin all my dreams?*

My husband and I were wrapping up our studies at university, looking at grad schools, planning to do mission work—all noble endeavors, yet not exactly baby-friendly. As weeks went by, I vacillated between two mindsets: *I am going to be the most creative and awesome mother ever—there is no way my progeny could be anything less than an unparalleled genius* versus *I've eaten nothing but cold cereal for the past week and can't even remember to let the dog out!*

My poor offspring's childhood memories will be riddled with disturbing scenes of my own ineptitude.

Tim, on the other hand, was completely calm and totally ready. Nothing caused him to worry or share my sense of sadness that our simple, child-free days were coming to an end.

As we tried to map out our future, some doors swung wide open and others slammed shut. It was almost calming to see things fall through sometimes. Then finally, a very obvious path was laid out clearly for us. Tim landed an incredible job which allowed me to take a year off and stay home. We moved out of our first apartment and into a beautiful house. Family happened to live close by and offered a great support system.

Though nothing went according to plan, in the end it was more than I ever thought we could achieve. It's nice to be amazed at what can happen when you say, *Jesus, Will you carry this, too?* and then let it go.

---

by Valarie DeLaVega Morse

Jenny and the Judges

What happened when I was 14 to the family that lived behind our home and how my mother responded to the drama taught me a lesson in Christian living.

The family consisted of a single mother and two daughters. Mary was quiet, complacent, and obedient. Jenny was headstrong and a bit on the wild side. Seemed like she was always getting in trouble. Nothing major; just sassy talk, sneaking out of church, short dresses. That kind of thing.

One summer, whisperings began: *What's up with the billowy dresses? What's with all the extra weight?* With the speculations, the story grew. Fourteen, I thrived on the next episode of *Jenny and Her Bastard Child*. I even asked my mother, the community socialite, to mingle and bring home the dirt. My mother was clearly disappointed. *It doesn't matter what the story is,* she said. *It's not our place to judge.*

A few weeks later, Jenny had her baby. There was no baby shower, no gifts, no visitors. The only ones there besides Jenny's mother and sister, were my mother and me. Jenny cried as she told us her story: She said she was married to a guy from Mauritius, but that he had to leave because his visa ran out. And that he promised to return.

As we walked home, I asked Mom if she believed that ridiculous story. She gave me the same look and said, *Even if we find it hard to believe, we should accept it as the truth. It's not our place to judge.*

Righteous blows continued. Jenny was banned from participating in church; she was shunned at community events; she was used as an example of what happens to bad teens. She couldn't even get a job! It seemed like everyone wanted her gone. That is, everyone, except my mother. She was always there to help Jenny—unconditionally. On the sidelines, I watched and learned the essence of Christ-likeness.

A year went by, two, and then three. Of course, there was no sign of the mysterious Mauritian husband. Then one day, out of nowhere, he arrived with his own bizarre story: A clerical mix-up in immigration landed him in prison with no way to contact Jenny.

The happy, reunited family quickly left for Mauritius and never returned. I waited for someone to admit they were wrong. Instead they asked, *What else could we do with no proof of a husband?*

My mother responded, *We could have chosen to be like Jesus.*

---

by Fylvia Fowler Kline

Oxymoron

We don't have a priest who is out of touch with our reality. He's been through weakness and testing, experienced it all—all but the sin. So let's walk right up to him and get what he is so ready to give. Take the mercy, accept the help. Hebrews 4:15-16

Living dead
Successful failure
Wimpy giant
Jumbo shrimp
Insecurely stable
Depressed Christian

A contradiction in terms.

Have you ever felt like that? As if you are made up of a spectrum of opposites—on one end one day and on the other the next? I've felt like that a lot lately. My head knows one thing and my heart feels another. And I'm trapped in darkness searching for level ground.

My prayers drop heavy from bouncing off brass; they pool cracked, bruised, broken all around my feet. But today I'm reminded of His contradictions.

His death brings life.
My less is His more.

My weakness brings His strength.

And I realize my incongruity means nothing to Him. He Himself was a paradox:

Fully God yet fully man,
He fulfilled law with grace.

He specializes in people like me. He knows what it's like to live between forces, to be pulled in opposite directions.

I am thankful I serve a God who understands, who is touched by the feelings of my infirmities. I'm letting His contradictions bring balance to mine today.

Join me.

Be encouraged today. You are never alone. He knows, He sees, He cares, and beyond that, He understands. He loves with an unfailing love and His grace is sufficient.

---

by Deidra Manning

Song of the Wind Chimes

Although quite windy, the weather was absolutely gorgeous. I had several errands to run, but they just had to wait. Nothing seemed more important at that moment than stopping to enjoy the arbitrary song of the wind chime.

The tune varied from gust to gust, but each was distinctly beautiful. I couldn't help but think: *Sing God a brand-new song! Earth and everyone in it, sing (Psalm 96:1).* My heart swelled with joy as I breathed in the fresh spring air and watched the trees dance to the song of the wind chime.

Then another pearl from God's Word came to mind: *So you'll go out in joy, you'll be led into a whole and complete life. The mountains and hills will lead the parade, bursting with song. All the trees of the forest will join the procession, exuberant with applause (Isaiah 55:12).*

While it is true that we are living in very disturbing times, we can live in confidence and say, *You'll welcome us with open arms when we run for cover to you. Let the party last all night! Stand guard over our celebration. You are famous, God, for welcoming*

God-seekers, for decking us out in delight (Psalm 5:11, 12).

I don't know about you, but that makes me want to sing for joy. My voice may not be beautiful, and sometimes my songs are nothing more than spontaneous words of praise, but that which is not perfect can be beautiful too, like the arbitrary song of a wind chime.

_____

by Susan Shimkovitz

Kibbles and Bits

My whole life has been invaded by pets of one kind or another, mostly dogs and cats. I even bird sat once. The experience scared me for life, but that's another story for another time. Back to pets. I am pleasantly surprised by the care God took when creating the animals that share our space. Inasmuch as they can be wildly violent, they can also be unconditionally loving.

Several years ago my mother brought two kittens home with her after a visit to grandma. When the kittens were introduced to Bandit, the family dog, he nibbled on their ears, scaring them almost to death. So naturally we named them after his favorite food, Kibbles and Bits. As much as Bits was friendly and rambunctious, Kibbles was reserved and cautious.

One afternoon Bits was trying to race the cars driving past our house. On her way back to our side of the street, she was too slow and was bumped and stunned by a car. My mother quickly picked her up and raced to the nearby veterinarian. Bits was given medication and spent the afternoon being cared for by the staff. When we brought her home later that evening, we placed her in a box lined with a soft blanket and small dishes of water and soft food. We kept a close eye on Bits, waiting to see any kind of improvement. What we didn't notice was Kibbles keeping a close eye on her as well. He spent many hours near her box, watching and waiting with us. Finally Kibbles decided he needed to be more proactive in Bits' recovery. So he disappeared for a few hours and returned with something he was sure Bits needed—a dead bird. He climbed into the box and laid it next to her. He spent the next several days as her constant companion, caring for her every need.

God has filled our lives with everyday reminders of how we should treat those around us; even our pets understand how much we need to love one another.

Oh, and by the way, Bits made a full recovery and lived happily ever after, away from the street and with her brother Kibbles as her constant companion.

by Cynthia Ward

The Pharisee and the Penny

The secret of perfect pizza and cinnamon rolls is in the dough. And I've never been able to get the dough quite right from scratch. Far away from modern grocers and frozen bread dough, it took 12-year-old Jenny to find a solution to my predicament: Buy dough instead of doughnuts.

After healing from the slap to my pride caused by a child solving my problem, I headed to the local doughnut shop. In my limited Nepali, I asked for uncooked doughnuts. Confusion spread from his wide eyes to his gaping mouth: *Do they eat dough? Use it as a prosthetic? Part of some kind of Christian puja?*

Just give me the dough! I exclaimed.

There was more confusion on his face—*How do I sell dough? By weight or handfuls?* His head swung from the big lump of dough dotted with flies to the freshly cut doughnuts ready to be fried, and from there, to my face. Pointing to the ones already cut, I said, *Just give me 20 of those.*

Squishing them all into one sticky ball, he stuffed them in a plastic bag. Later in my kitchen, the 20 uncooked doughnuts quickly converted into a large pizza and a dozen cinnamon rolls. It was wonderful. Picking up the phone, I spread the word. Soon everyone on campus was at the doughnut shop! But alas, the doughnut guy wised up. Overnight the price of 20 uncooked doughnuts more than doubled!

Furious, I was ready for war. I had a strategy in place to put the doughnut guy out of business. He picked the wrong person to mess with! In my fuming rage over being gypped, there was no room for compassion for the simpleton making a living, no tolerance for haphazard economics, no appreciation for the dough I couldn't make myself, no common sense to nudge me to realize it wasn't battle-worthy.

It's the principle of the thing! I said in my defense when my family pointed out that I was fighting over an increase of a penny per doughnut. In my rage, I forgot the primary purpose for being in Nepal—to show Christ through my words, my deeds and my relationships.

In my rage, I boycotted the doughnut shop for a whole year. In retrospect, it was more about the Pharisee than about the principle in me—focusing anything and everything, except love.

---

by Fylvia Fowler Kline

The Opposite of Trust

Trust is a lot like driving. Most roads are marked with solid or dotted lines to indicate the side of the road cars should drive on. Every day hundreds of thousands of people drive up and down highways never once stopping to think about what would happen if oncoming traffic failed to stay on its side of the painted line.

Even though we know that the line can be crossed at any moment, we drive with ease, placing our trust in a simple painted line. Yet how difficult it is to continuously place our trust in the hands of the Father!

Trusting in the Lord is a big step of faith and should come to us as naturally as breathing. There is no reason to doubt that God would ever fail us. He'd never cross the line. Yet, fears and doubts get in the way and we often fail to trust God 100 per cent.

A key to breaking through the doubts and fears is to remember that *there is no room in love for fear. Well-formed love banishes fear* (I John 4:18). And in God there is no fear, no doubt and no indecision. Identifying your feelings of fear and understanding that fear is not of God will break you free and help you seek the peace of God.

Throughout Scripture are verses of comfort, encouragement and reassurance for times when you are tormented by fear. Read these, memorize some and build your defense against fear.

Exodus 14:13
Deuteronomy 31:6
Joshua 1:9
Psalm 23:4
Psalm 27:1
Isaiah 41:13
Jeremiah 29:11
Luke 1:30
Luke 2:10
John 14:27
Hebrews 13:6
2 Timothy 1:7.

_____

by Amanda Johnson

Too Busy to Stop

Call for help when you're in trouble—I'll help you, and you'll honor me. Psalm 50:15

From her voice, I knew something was terribly wrong. But she wouldn't tell me over the phone. She insisted on coming over. I hurried out to meet her. When she saw me, she blurted, *Leang Eng Pheng met with an accident and is no more!*

I stared at her, too dazed to speak. Only one thought flashed in my mind: I was too late.

Two days earlier I had heard that he wasn't keeping well. I made a mental note to visit him. But in my busyness, I forgot. And now he was gone, before I could find the time.

Eng was a joy to have in my class. He was the eager beaver, frontbencher, always burning with questions. Being a thoughtful and generous young man, when he passed my ESL class, he bought me a gift from his summer job.

Eng and I were more than teacher and student. During one of his visits to my office, Eng told me he liked me because I reminded him of his mom. He had even grown to love my Indian cooking and would take my food to his mom. And when he'd return from visiting his mother, he would flood my desk with large baskets of fresh fruit. Now, there would be no more visits from Eng.

How many times has my busyness gotten in the way of making time for the people in my life? I should know better, been better—especially when I have a loving Father who is never too busy for me. He is just a prayer away.

_____

by Alvina Kullu Sulankey

Divine Appointment

I didn't want to be in the middle seat, wedged between two strangers on a cross-country flight. I was tired from the intense business of the last few days and just wanted to be able to sleep. But God had a divine appointment for me.

My seatmate to the right radiated nervous energy. Thick dark curls and large black eyes contrasted with her pale olive complexion. We chatted easily as she laid out the panorama of her broken life before me.

Born to Jewish parents who were too young, Amelie grew up being shuttled between her two grandmothers in Morocco and Tunisia. And when one of them moved to Israel, Amelie moved with her. Somehow, between all that moving around, she managed to study music and hook up with a band.

By 35, her nomadic, rock singer life had taken her all over the world. And now was she was moving from California for the fourth time, leaving her husband of five years, to live with an aunt on Long Island.

At first she bantered superficially, as if her life had been an exciting adventure. But as we talked on through the long hours, she became more reflective and we began to converse on a heart level. I prayed for wisdom to reach through the pain and place this hurting child in God's lap.

You must struggle with your sense of identity, I gently probed.

I'm always trying to find myself, she admitted.

Then God-given words began to flow from my lips and she drank them like a thirsty traveler. *You are precious to God,* I heard myself say. *Your identity is not in what you do or what you have or where you live or what you look like. Your identity is in God. He has plans for your future. He can give you hope.* By the end of the trip, her face had softened like that of a little girl and she hugged me tightly.

A few days later, I got an email from Amelie. She had fasted and prayed for God's guidance as she returned back to Him.

What's your middle seat, the place you don't want to be, the situation you are avoiding, the call you refuse to take? Take that seat, and you'll find something far greater than a chance to turn your head and sleep.

---

by Brenda Kis

Beat the Heat

Those who live near him will be blessed by him, be blessed and prosper like golden grain. Hosea 14:7

The power of the sun beating down on the earth is oppressive. Every living thing wilts as dehydration begins. Leaves and flowers dip their heads as moisture evaporates. Animals seek shade in an effort to find relief. Even the movements and thoughts of people slow down and become labored.

The heat of sin has the same effect as the sun does on earth. Sin bears down on us, causing a struggle in our efforts to rise above it and live. We become weary, trying to fight it in a demanding world. We become discouraged in our seemingly useless efforts. Sometimes sadly, we give up altogether and lose the battle.

Watering my garden, I sense an analogy. The water refreshes the plants, just as surely as it revives birds and humans. Diving into water on hot, sultry days, we revel in the cooling comfort and return for another dip and another and another.

The comfort of spiritual refreshment is long-lasting and benefits us physically. We are totally rejuvenated with an infilling of sustaining energy when we accept the water of life from the Son of God. His cathartic renewal lasts forever, sustaining us from day to day.

Our God is far greater than the power of the sun. He is the maker of all things and He knows us and He knows sin better than anyone else. Only He can redeem us and bring us to a safe place, a place of rest. His Word refreshes and energizes us to see beyond our trials and move forward, one step at a time, in new directions.

In the heat of life, there is a place where we can triumph. It is under the shadow of the Almighty. When the heat becomes too much to bear, we don't have to wither and die, we don't have to give up. God is the One to follow and Jesus is the Way to rise above trials and survive. The water of life helps us to come clean, in whatever situation we find ourselves.

We can survive when we cling to God's promise, *When I looked again and saw what he was doing, I decided to heal him, lead him, and comfort him* (Isaiah 57:18).

---

by Patricia Day

For Loot or Love

Yes! Come, Master Jesus. Revelation 22: 20

Sky's favorite thing to do as a toddler was to look through Grandma's silk saris. The brilliance of the bright colors and gold embroidery would keep her enthralled for hours. And she was ecstatic when she learned that all of them would be hers one day.

However, she did not understand why she couldn't have them right away if one day they were all going to be hers anyway. It became obvious that it was time to have a discussion on the subject of death and inheritance. Unfortunately, the talk had no effect on her.

She focused only on the loot and not on Grandma's love.

With great impatience, she'd ask us every day, *When is Grandma going to die?*

I wonder if in describing heaven to His disciples, Jesus was trying to ease the pain of separation? Somehow knowing that Jesus is preparing a fabulous gold and diamond studded resort, keeps us motivated to keep going in this far from perfect world. An entire chapter of Revelation describes this wonderland—gold walls, bejeweled mansions, delicious, unending supply of food (In my conjuring of heaven, I've added chocolate to the staple diet).

After that big tease of the taste of heaven, the Bible ends with Jesus assuring us of two things: 1) That His coming is a certainty; and 2) That He is coming quickly. And John the Revelator responds, *Come Lord Jesus.*

For sure, our response ought to be the same as John's–*Come, Lord Jesus.* Yet I wonder if my *Come Lord Jesus* has the same reason behind it as John's did. Am I wishing of the Second Coming because I want to be with Jesus or because I want to claim my inheritance?

We should revisit, every day, the reason behind our response, our longing for Jesus' return. Do we yearn the Second Coming for the loot—the perfect world and the perfect life? Or for the desire to be with the One we love?

For loot or love, what's it to be?

---

by Fylvia Fowler Kline

Hindsight

Hindsight is the best vision to have. It helps us learn from our challenges, our errors and our faulty human nature. It also gives us insight into why things often turn out the way they do.

I first experienced the value of hindsight when I was 14. I was a runaway, living a drug-fueled life on the streets of Chicago. Somewhere inside of me, I knew that was not the life I envisioned for myself. It was not the life I wanted, but I did what I had to do to feed my habit and to survive.

My home was the streets for two years before the law finally caught up with me and I ended up in a group home for youth in Bartlett, Illinois. It was a large home in an old convent with about 40 boys and girls and not enough staff to supervise all of us. And for the first time in my life, I was truly afraid. Most of the kids there were hardened to the core. They were mean and angry and cold-hearted—a consequence of being tossed aside and abused all their lives, just as I was. Yet, I never saw myself becoming like them one day.

One day, group of us were walking down to the old well house on the property. It was a large well house with a door and was big enough to hold a person. One of the boys, maybe about 14 years old, was following behind us cool kids. Mentally challenged and lacking in maturity, he followed us even though he didn't belong. Looking at him and then at the well house, the group turned on him like a pack of wolves. With abusive words and shoves they made sure he knew he didn't belong.

The boy stooped low, crying and begging that we just let him walk with us. I was angry at his submissive behavior. *He should stand tall and strong and not show signs of weakness,* I thought to myself.

Taking his crying as a sign of their victory, they dragged him into the well house and locked him in. I stood there and watched the abuse and said nothing. I didn't come to his aid. I just stood there and allowed it to happen.

At that moment, I realized I was the weak one. At that moment, I saw a me I didn't like and I never wanted to be like that again. That moment haunts me to this day.

In hindsight, it was an experience that made me look deep inside of me and vow to change my heart.

---

by Laurie Owen

When God Goes to Seattle

But even if mothers forget, I'd never forget you—never. Look, I've written your names on the backs of my hands. Isaiah 49:15-16

We lived near Seattle and often visited Pike Place Market. Walking through the place one day, engrossed in all the things that caught our attention, I suddenly realized that I'd forgotten to uncover Kylie's cage. Plus I hadn't fed her or refilled her bowl with water.

Kylie was our affectionate cockatiel. She trusted me to care for her. She knew that every morning I would uncover her cage to bring in the light of a new day and give her food and water. I could hardly enjoy my lunch thinking about my sweet little bird sitting in the dark. She was probably lonely and hungry and anxious about the cats peeking up at her from under the blanket.

When we got home, even before we unlocked the door, we could hear Kylie. But it wasn't the noisy chirping of a stressed out bird or the squawking sound of scolds. Instead, it was the sound of Kylie singing her heart out. Despite a dark cage with no food or water and with two prowling cats, her hopeful heart seemed full of faith that I would return and feed her. It humbled me to realize I was God to that little bird.

Life on earth can get pretty dark. Sometimes grief and pain throw a blanket over our joy. We get hungry and lonely and we feel the breath of the enemy surrounding us. But even when the sun is hidden by clouds and we can't see God at work in our lives, we need to have faith and trust that God is there.

We can have faith like a trusting little bird. Sometimes it may seem like God is off gallivanting in Seattle. At times like this, we need to remember how reliable He's been in the past—and we need to sing of our past victories and joy even in the darkest hours of life.

Look at the birds of the air, they do not sow or reap or store away in barns, and yet your heavenly father feeds them. Are you not much more valuable than they are (Matthew 6:26)?

---

by Cherilyn Clough

Mother's Love

What marvelous love the Father has extended to us! Just look at it—
we're called children of God! That's who we really are. I John 3:1

I called a dear friend today. She is 90 years old and
has many children, grandchildren, great-
grandchildren and even a few great-great
grandchildren.

We began our conversation with the usual
pleasantries. As we chatted, our dialogue drifted
towards things of great consequence. She shared that
she was excited to one day see her son again. He has
been gone a year now. We paused to ponder how
wonderful the Second Coming would be. I could hear
her smile through the telephone as she envisioned
seeing her son again and being with Jesus.

Suddenly, her voice changed. Her speech became
hoarse and broken. Tears surely flowed down her
weathered face. When she spoke again, I was
surprised by her words. In a clear voice she said,
Tonya, pray for my daughter. I was filled with
astonishment and wonder. My dear friend had not
been crying for her son whose life had been cut short.
Instead she was praying for her daughter who was
lost.

This mother has been praying for her wayward daughter for over 50 years. *How many restless nights has she cried out to God to save her precious child?* I wondered.

In her silence, I felt her pain and heard her anxious cry, *Who will pray for my daughter when I am gone?*

A mother's love is a poignant reflection of God's love for us. Jesus desires each of us to be with Him. He does not want one single child missing from His flock. Urgently, He is pleading. With outstretched arms, He calls. If you are a lost child, hear His voice. Answer His call.

If you are a mother desperately pleading for a child who is adrift, take comfort. Jesus is doing whatever it takes to touch your child's heart.

---

by Tonya Mechling

Measuring Time

How you measure time often depends on where you are in life, what drives you mad or wild, your goals or lack of goals. If you are pregnant, time is marked by the girth of your belly that indicates another week has gone by. If you are writing your first novel, time is measured by word count or chapter.

Where I am in life, with my last child away at college, I measure time in a strange yet meaningful way—by rows of strawberry stitches. When I found this particularly beautiful pattern for a scarf, I decided to make one for Sky. The pattern used chunky wool, a fat hook and boasted itself as a weekend project. But I replaced the wool with fine cotton and the fat hook with a slender 0.65 mm stainless steel. The result was the beginnings of an intricate lace scarf made up of delicate rows of strawberry stitches. Unfortunately, my adaptation of the original pattern is going to cost me months, if not years, of time to complete it.

It should annoy me. But it doesn't. It's a labor of love* for my daughter. As I crochet, millimeter by millimeter in length, my mind and heart fill up with memories of me being her mom and she being my daughter.

The making of this scarf has become my measure of time—not just of the present, but of the past as well. And in that measurement, in my remembering, I feel blessed—very blessed.

also turns out to be good exercise for arthritic joints.

_____

by Fylvia Fowler Kline

Nail Polish Mess

I have this weird habit . . . or maybe it's an obsession. I don't know. But I can never seem to leave my nails painted all the same color for more than a week.

Last night as I was working on a midterm, I spotted a couple of bottles of nail polish on my dresser and started going to town on my nails. The result was each hand with pinkies painted white with pink tips and multi-colored sparkles; the ring fingers black with purple and blue sparkles; the middle ones black with silver sparkles; the index white with multi-colored sparkles; and the thumbs white with multi-colored sparkles and purple tips covered in blue sparkles.

My nails are definitely wayyyy different than they were a week ago.

My life should be like my nails, I say. God doesn't want me to stay the same. He wants me to be in a constant stay of changing, growing, advancing.

My current paint job may seem like nothing more than a hot mess. But that's okay because I think it's awesome. Similarly, I may not like the changes I'm going through, but that's okay because it's where God wants me to be and He thinks I'm awesome.

Change is good, especially when we are changing—
slowly, daily—into His image.

by Heather Joy Vires

And the Deaf Shall Hear

He's done it all and done it well. He gives hearing to the deaf, speech to the speechless. Mark 7:37

It was my second pregnancy. Everything was going well until seven or eight weeks before my due date, when I went into labor. I barely made it to the hospital before my baby was born—all 4 pounds, 12 ounces of her.

A couple of months later, the baby woke up crying. When I reached into the crib to pick her up, she opened her eyes, looking very startled. At that very moment, I knew my baby had not heard me come into the room nor heard the sound of my voice or the rustling of the sheets as I reached in to pick her up.

The next day, when I took her in for a regular checkup, I told the doctor of my suspicions. Taking two metal canister lids, he banged them together behind my baby. She didn't hear a thing. A hearing specialist was brought in and he too confirmed that she was totally deaf.

I felt as though I had gone into the hospital with a perfect baby, but had left with another. I later learned this was part of a normal grieving process. But at that time, this added enormous guilt over my already negative reactions and thoughts.

On my way home, I stopped to visit Penny, a friend with a mentally challenged sister and whose faith and strength I admire. With her, I let go of all my feelings—I cried and I got angry; I was hurt and I was overwhelmed. I was convinced I had made a grave mistake and my daughter's deafness was the punishment. But through Penny's gentle understanding, she helped me see that the deafness was a birth defect, nothing more and nothing less. My baby was still the same beautiful child, a gift from God.

I was finally ready to face my family and be the strongest advocate I could be for my new baby. Little did I know the obstacles that would test my faith. But I continued hanging on to God and His promises. As my love for God deepened, I began to find ways to communicate with my baby and help her become a loving, productive Christian woman.

I have learned so much through her. Looking back, I realize she is my perfect child. She has taught me the true meaning of God's patient love.

Jesus is coming back to take us home (John 14:1-3). I want to be there when the first sound my daughter hears is the sweet voice of Jesus calling her home.

---

by Vicky Tibbetts

The Headache

Call to me and I will answer you. I'll tell you marvelous and wondrous things that you could never figure out on your own. Jeremiah 33:3

After traveling four hours to speak at a women's meeting, I had a raging headache. As I sat in the front row waiting my turn at the microphone, I held my pain-filled head in my hands, too sick to care if people noticed. Worried about my ability to speak, I sent an SOS prayer up to the Lord. *There's no way I can walk up there. You have to help me.*

Through the music worship and other formalities, the pain increased. I felt like a steel band had been rammed over my head. I stayed seated during the singing, wondering if I should have the person next to me inform the leader that I was too sick to speak. But just as I was about to do that, a thought seemed to drop into my tormented mind: *When your name is called, stand up and the headache will disappear.*

One hour into the meeting, my headache in full throttle, the preliminaries had finally ended. It was time. I heard the leader say many kind things about me, but I couldn't even raise my head to acknowledge them. The pain was that bad.

Finally, I heard the invitation, the cue for me to get out of my chair, and walk to the stage. At the mention of my name, the band of pain loosened up. I stood up and began walking to the platform. With each step, the pain subsided. By the time I reached the microphone, the pain had vanished.

God could've relieved me of pain an hour earlier. I know I would have appreciated that. But sometimes He lets us experience human frailties to the point that we have no choice but to depend completely on Him to fix the situation.

When weakness rules and our only option is to trust Him, we rediscover His amazing power.

---

by Rose McCormick Brandon

Small Talk to Big Gestures

I was sitting next to a stranger, in a room full of more strangers, waiting for a meeting to begin. And like all well-mannered, cultured people, the stranger next to me and I exchanged names and proceeded to engage in small talk.

In some weird turn of this particular conversational event, the subject turned from volunteerism to garlic. Yes, garlic. Matt began to tell me about his annual project: He plants 5000 heads of garlic; nurtures, cultivates and harvests them; hangs them to dry; and then gives them to friends and soup kitchens.

Intrigued and somewhat floored by Matt's unique hobby, I had nothing left in my pocket of small talk except to say, *I like garlic and often pickle it.* This led him to tell me about his wife's role in Project Garlic— She pickles garlic as gifts for others!

I'm sure I would have learned of other fascinating ways Matt and his wife are involved in their community had it not been time for the meeting to begin. At the end of the meeting, Matt and I exchanged the usual, expected pleasantries, said we'd trade samples of pickled garlic sometime and then bade each other goodbye.

122

We've all had such encounters—We meet people we find interesting or with whom we have much in common. When we part, we make a mental note of following up, keeping in touch, blah blah blah. Then life catches by with us, and we don't email, let alone share our pickled garlic. I didn't expect this encounter to be any different.

But then, the next day, guess who stopped by? And guess what he brought for me? Matt and the jar of pickled garlic remind me of how little effort it takes to be a person of compassion, purpose and good will.

In that one gesture, Matt did what all human beings are capable of, but what only a few take the time to do. He flipped from stranger to friend.

The next time you meet someone, try finding a way to flip them from stranger to friend.

---

by Fylvia Fowler Kline

Treads of Truth

It's going to cost $745.35, but that includes installation. These are good tires, not like the ones you now have. It's a good deal. A good deal? Sounds more like disappointment than a good deal.

Once again my estimate and budget were thrown out the window. Once more my plans had fallen through. We were never going to get things paid off with such unexpected expenses popping up. The orthodontist appointment was Thursday; I could imagine what that was going to cost! I had already been forewarned that all three children needed braces.

As my thoughts became more and more obsessive, God stopped me in my tracks. Gently and quietly, He weeded through my thoughts with His probing, questioning truth: *Are you mad about the tires with metal exposed? Aren't these the ones your husband noticed by coincidence? Are you mad because getting new tires means you have to skip anniversary plans for which you saved money? Are you so angry that these are the same tires I've made last this long, that these are the same tires that I kept from blowing out? Are you really angry about how I've kept you safe when you've been too busy running around to keep an eye on your very old and worn out tires?*

Of course, God is right, I reflected back in childish embarrassment. He has kept us safe in that car for only He knows how long. I was focusing on the immediate cost and the added debt, without looking at the big picture.

A closer look and I saw what my self-centeredness had blinded me thus far: I saw my family in God's big hands. I saw the furrow lines, like ridged little paths that keep us in place. I saw the cupped sides like a protective hedge around us.

With that picture I remembered that I couldn't plan life. I can never come up with enough contingencies to cover the unexpected. I need to focus on what I know and what I've experienced of God. He is my source, and if He has kept me this far, I'm pretty sure He's got me covered the rest of the way.

_____

by Deidra Manning

Ungrateful Birthday Girl

I have now reached my forties and am currently sliding recklessly into my mid-forties. I'm not really all that happy about it. I can say that I do not care much for birthdays any more. I am in agony when I have to stand (or sit) and smile while *Happy Birthday* is being sung to me.

Today a co-worker is enjoying the joys of a birthday celebrated on a school campus. I sit and listen as a group of twenty-five 1st and 2nd grade students sing Happy Birthday at the top of their lungs. With big smiles, they clap and giggle. You can just see the look of pure joy in their eyes as they wish him a happy birthday. For them this is the best day of the year— well this and Christmas. They're thinking, *What's not to love about a birthday? Party, good. Cake, good. Presents, really good!*

This makes me ponder on what it is that makes me not enjoy my birthday these days. After all, I did when I was six. Objectively, I stripped my birthdays and acknowledged the things about my mid-life birthdays that are still good.

1. I am happy to be part of the human race for another year.

2. I appreciate the calls from friends and family who remember my special day.
3. A homemade cake from Mom's oven makes me smile at memories of many, and I mean MANY, previous birthdays.

You know the Ten Commandments have a place for birthdays. It says, *Honor your father and mother so that you'll live a long time in the land that God, your God, is giving you (Exodus 20:12, NIV)*. See, right there it says if you're nice to your parents, plenty of birthdays will come your way. Okay, so maybe it is a bit more complicated than that. But I think it means when we live a life that honors our parents, we live a life of service to everyone around us. And such a life will be given the gift of eternal birthdays in Heaven. You know, the place God is preparing for us.

So maybe when my birthday rolls around again, I'll spend the time being a six-year-old and really enjoy it. Party, good. Lemon cake, good. Another year to honor my parents and be of service to others, really good.

---

by Cynthia Ward

Coming Home

It was beautiful! Tall towering pines lined the drive.
Rocky beds covered with soft moss decorated the
landscape. Wild animals frolicked in the meadow. The
cottage was carefully placed amongst the bountiful
display of God's handiwork. It was our dream home.
We toured the property and signed the lease. We just
had to wait three weeks before we could move in.

My husband and I dreamed. We planned. We
researched and spent a lot time looking at the
pictures of the house on the Internet. Three weeks
seemed like forever. We talked about how wonderful
it was going to be to finally move in. Each day
seemed to drag. As we imagined ourselves living in
the little cottage, our present accommodations
become increasingly intolerable. Anticipating the
move became central to our lives.

On moving day, as I breathed in the lovely scenery, I
was reminded of another home, one more beautiful
and magnificent than anything I can conjure up. Jesus
said, *There is plenty of room for you in my Father's
home. If that weren't so, would I have told you that
'I'm on my way to get a room ready for you?'*
(John 14:2).

One day we are going to look up in the clouds and see Jesus with His retinue of angels. He is going to beckon His people to come home! Oh how I yearn for that day!

Although we are not in our heavenly mansions yet, we can still enjoy beauty here on earth. The joy I feel as I walk through the forest or dance in the meadow by my little cottage is just a taste of what heaven will be like. The awe I feel when I watch His creatures is a glimpse of the wonder I am going to experience when I play with the animals in heaven.

God wants us to find blessings and joy in nature. He bids us to come home in Him.

---

by Tonya Mechling

Stinger in the Tongue

For the despairing man, there should be kindness from his friend. Job 6:14, The New American Standard

Today a wasp got trapped in my living room. In desperation he dashed himself from window to ceiling to furniture. I could have simply and politely held the front door open and let him fly into freedom. But in my fear, I began running around the room flailing my arms at him—which didn't help the situation. It ended when Roy came to my rescue with a blue fly swatter and smacked the wasp against the windowsill.

As I watched him twitching to death, I remembered another wasp incident many years ago. Wrinkles, our part Sharpei, part Chow, part Lab, part whatever dog, had just joined our family. A reject at the puppy farm she was way past puppyhood and well into defiant puberty. She had a mind of her own and did as she pleased. Surrounded by woods, strange animals and insects, our home was doggy heaven. One muggy summer day, a wasp that was trying to enter our home got smacked down by my husband and lay twitching on the porch. Wrinkles went diving towards the wasp. In spite of the many commands to *stay,* she lunged forward and took the dying wasp in her mouth. In desperation, the wasp attempted one

130

last victory before being chewed to death. He stung Wrinkles in her tongue! With a yelp Wrinkles began running around in circles, alternately grating her tongue against her front teeth and sticking her paw in her mouth. But the stinger was firmly and painfully implanted in her pink and black Sharpei-wannabe tongue. No way could she take the stinger out of her mouth by herself. It took three of us. Jez sat on her to hold her down and Roy held her mouth open while I used a pair of tweezers.

Lesson learned that day by dog and family: Some things we just can't do by ourselves. You're better off accepting help from others.

And there's nothing wrong with that.

_____

by Fylvia Fowler Kline

The Perfect Rose Garden

A child from a broken home, I was not a happy girl. My father abandoned me when my parents divorced. Then, too overwhelmed with her own grief, my mother farmed us out to several relatives. Most of the time I lived with my grandparents. When they needed a break, they'd ship me off to another relative's home for a while.

One summer day I landed at a great aunt's summer house on the lake. She was older, pleasantly plump and wore a large straw hat as she cared for her roses that surrounded her back deck. To me it was the perfect setting for a tea party.

And that's what we did. We had a tea party. First we went to the lake and she showed me how to pick wild mint for the tea. Then we poached eggs and made toast while the mint tea brewed.

Sitting outside on that perfect morning in her beautiful rose garden, I felt the happiest I had ever been. Someone had taken the time to make me feel special, to give me some attention. I hold that perfect moment close to my heart to this day. Her name was Aunt Rose Marie; I named my daughter after her even though I never saw Aunt Rose Marie again.

It's strange how precious moments are preserved in our minds. I still remember the white arched trellis and the red roses growing over it. I remember the taste of her fresh mint tea. And I don't recall ever having better poached eggs again. If I close my eyes and take a deep breath, I can smell Aunt Rose Marie's roses and see her chubby pink cheeks smiling at me from under that straw hat.

There's another perfect place where I will be loved and cherished and where I will walk in the perfect rose garden with my heavenly Father. But until then, tea time and the smiles with others will fill my heart.

_____

by Laurie Owen

Spring Into Action

Adam was a gardener, and God, who made him, sees that half of all gardening is done upon the knees.—Rudyard Kipling

I'm a country girl at heart and love my garden with a passion.

The rich dark soil running through my hands is rather therapeutic to me. There is just something incredibly wonderful in knowing that vigorous new life will soon spring forth from the dirt, and that I will play a pivotal role in that process.

No matter how much time I spend in my garden, I never cease to be amazed at the miracle of life. When I see a teeny seedling breaking through the ground, I marvel at how it assumes the posture of praise—tiny new leaves stretched heavenward towards the light. And when I see this, all the time and effort I spent preparing the soil and tending to the seed, is forgotten in the same way a mother's labor pains vanish when she sees the face of her newborn.

I imagine our heavenly Father feels much the same way each time a soul climbs out of this world's dirt and reaches for His light. God does not need us to help tend His garden, yet He has given us the privilege of doing so until He gathers His harvest.

God's children all have a hand in planting the gospel seed and watering it, until vigorous life springs forth Finally, brethren, let us not neglect to pray. If we are to see a harvest for God's kingdom, this is the most important part of our labor (I Corinthians 3:5-9).

by Susan Shimkovitz

Leave It

Leave it in God's hands is a phrase that has made its way in and out of my life on many different occasions. I've used it to encourage a friend in times of distress. The phrase reminds me that God is in control.

But when a friend recently used the phrase on me when I was experiencing high anxiety and stress in my life, my first reaction was, *How is that supposed to help. I need answers now!*

I'm not proud of my response. In the midst of crisis, I wanted to hear words of action and direction. Obviously, I was only hearing the *leave it* part of the phrase. As a result, my reaction was disappointment and frustration. I should have been focusing on where I needed to leave my burden — *in God's hands.*

We often seek advice that calls for some kind of action and momentum — go, fix, adjust, regroup. The concept of just *leaving it* contradicts our need to be in control, to be in charge.

But in the life of a true Christian, it's God and not the person who is in charge.

Leaving it may seem like a non-action plan, but instead it is the most effective step of action we can take. Stepping away, sitting still before God (Psalm 46:10), and giving things over to Him in prayer brings greater power into the circumstance than we could possibly do ourselves.

Philippians 4:6 encourages us, *Don't fret or worry. Instead of worrying, pray. Let petitions and praises shape your worries into prayers, letting God know your concerns.*

What a great reminder to trust God and to leave it in His hands

---

by Amanda Johnson

The Best Kind of Rainbow

The kids and I were tagging along on one of Roy's business road trips. This time it was Maryland's eastern shore. Roy was done with his appointments earlier than expected, so we wandered southward, following the bay, from Crisfield towards Virginia.

As we drove into Bloxom, the earthy call of homesteading and simplicity was magnetic. Before we knew it, we were looking at real estate books and making plans to move to the country and homeschool the kids. We even found the perfect home—Every bedroom had a fireplace and a balcony that overlooked the bay; a separate wing that begged to be converted into a school-house; and two guard geese in the front yard that had a reputation for hissing and biting intruders. It was simply perfect. As we pulled out of the driveway and headed down the sandy road back towards the highway, we saw what we dubbed as our perfect double rainbow.

It's a sign, we decided. We were going to sell our home and move to the country. In our daydreaming, we saw ourselves wielding walking sticks and pitchforks, donning practical dungarees during the day and purchasing rockers and wind chimes for our wrap-around, front porch country living. But when we got back to our city life, objectivity and obligations set in and we scratched our plans along with our daydreaming. It was no big deal; just one of those *c'est la vie* moments where nothing's lost or gained. Every now and then, over the years, one of us recollects that perfect rainbow and our silly plans to move to the country. We smile and move on with life.

Almost a decade later one day, I saw a different kind of rainbow on my drive home. It was a tiny fistful of bright cheer tenaciously pushing itself through the dark, puffy folds of an angry thunderstorm. The little thing just wouldn't give up. Every time a furious wind whipped the grey clouds into a darker shade of rage, the rainbow just shoved its cheery head in between and out for any one to see. Fascinated, I pulled over and watched. As I watched the determined rainbow, I changed my mind. This rainbow is now my favorite. It reminds of everything I've lost and everything I've gained. And like my tenacious burst of rainbow, Goodness and Grace have abounded even in the darkest times.

---

by Fylvia Fowler Kline

Bug Squashing

If he stumbles, he's not down for long; God has a grip on his hand.
Psalm 37:24

My 30-minute walk ended 15 minutes early when I stepped on a scary looking half-spider, half-tick, part-crab, part-monster, creepy-crawly creature. My leisurely walk quickly turned into an out-and-out sprint back towards my car.

After I settled down (okay, I admit, I never really settled down!), I decided I could never take those shoes home with me. Oh, I know I could wash them in bleach, dry them in the purifying sun and it'd be back to business as usual, but I was not about being realistic at that moment. Remembering I had an extra pair of shoes in the trunk of my car, my plan was to change shoes. Immediately.

As I approached the car, I calmed down and curiosity got the better of me. Now I just had to go back and see the crushed remains of the creature. Slowly approaching the point of demise, I was shocked at what I found. The creature had somehow dragged itself out of harm's way and was nowhere to be found.

The tenacity of the creature made me smile. It taught me a lesson too: Even when we fall on the hardest of times, we need to keep moving forward, no matter what. Sometimes the enemy knocks us down and sprints away happy about our predicament. But when we trust in God, no matter how far we have fallen, we can get back up again!

---

by Ruth-Ann Thompson

Fear

I came so they can have real and eternal life, more and better life than they ever dreamed of. John 10:10

In the warm, humid summers of the South, crickets grow big, black and shiny. Hearing the cricket sing didn't bother me, but when they made their way into my house, I suddenly had a problem—a big, hoppy problem.

When my children were little and my husband travelled a lot, I had to catch the crickets that found their way into our home. And I was afraid of crickets.

Whenever I assembled my cricket catcher (a disposable cup and a thin, sturdy piece of cardboard), feelings of trepidation would wash over me. What if the cricket turned around and jumped in my face, or attacked me with its stinger? Now don't quote me on the ability of crickets to sting. From where I was and from the size of the long, black pokey things protruding out of their faces, it sure looked like they could do some major damage to my delicate skin.

One day my boys brought from the library books on insects—on crickets, specifically. Reading about them with my boys, something incredible happened. My fear of crickets began to diminish. The more I

142

understood that the cricket's goal in life was not to attack me with its stinger and the more I learned the use of the stinger, the less I feared the cricket.

I learned that the stinger was actually an egg dropper that the females used to poke into the dirt and deposit their eggs. Whew! Gaining knowledge and understanding about what I was facing helped take away my fears.

Later, someone explained fear to me as an acronym: False Evidence Appearing Real. That was certainly applicable to my fear of crickets.

God's been dealing with my other fears. I've discovered that when we don't walk in the truth about something, those lies have the potential to breed a fear that can be paralyzing.

Ask God to help you reveal the irrational fears that may have you bound and paralyzed. Then let the truth of God's presence and control help you overcome those fears.

_____

by Debra Torres

Mother: Looking Glass

You know the nursery rhyme *What are little girls made of? Sugar and spice and everything nice.* That wasn't me. I was more like the little girl who *when good was very good but when she was bad, was horrid.* Except that I was hardly ever good.

My earliest memory is the loss of some precious candy. My mother offered me a piece of candy, but I wanted two. Insisting it was one or nothing, she gave me till the count of three to take it or lose it. When she got to three, she popped the candy in her mouth and walked away. There was no reasoning, no second chance, no saving the candy for later. I quickly learned that second chances are rare and that stubbornness is self destructive.

My mother saw potential in me, though. She taught me to channel my headstrong spirit in positive directions. And even in discipline, my mother was my best friend. She has always been there for me, kept my secrets, shared my giggles.

And in my best friend, I met God. Growing up, I often heard my mother talking out aloud to God. She'd say stuff like *Now you've got to see it from my point of view* or *If you think I can do one more thing today, you've just got to show me how.* Or when she was frustrated, I'd hear her say *I'm not going to stop bugging you until you show me how this makes sense.* She did a lot of praying on her knees. But most of the time she just talked to Him as if He were standing right next to her.

Yes, my mother taught me a lot of things. But most important of all, through her I felt the first warm touch of God's love. I was a horrid little girl, but because of my mom and her partnership with God, I think I turned out pretty good after all.

_____

by Fylvia Fowler Kline

They Tried Me

They watched me at work among them, as over and over they tried my patience. Psalm 95:9

I pleaded. I cried, *Please Lord, answer my prayer.* This burden was too heavy. I had been carrying it for almost a year now. Throughout each day, I would ask God to share His plan for my life. I truly felt like I was going through a Moses-in-the-desert experience.

Would this burden always be with me? During my most worrisome hours, God would remind me of Joseph locked away in prison. I imagined David hiding in the wilderness. Gently, God told Moses, David and Joseph how to deliver His flock from destruction. Through God, they were able to accomplish the impossible. All three men went through dark times so that they could be prepared to do God's great work.

As I contemplated my worries and fears, God spoke to me through Psalm 95. The Israelites had seen great and mighty works. A sea being parted, manna from heaven, victory from enemies. These were all miraculous examples of God's protection. Surely they should have known better than to doubt Him when times got tough! Verse 9 has an almost inconsequential phrase, *They watched me at work among them.* As I was just about to launch into a mental lecture against the Israelites, God halted my condemnation; *My precious child, Tonya, you too have seen my works.*

My life is filled with blessings, miracles and amazing testimonies of God. Yes! He is alive in my life. I have seen His work. His love never fails. He never abandons. His arms are always wrapped around me. He has taken my hand and led me through the precarious moments of life. I may not know what the future holds, but I do know that God does have a plan.

I fully put my trust back in Him.

Lord, today I ask you to take away my doubts and worries. Remind me of all that you have done in my life. Never let me feel superior to others going through hardship. Whether in prison, in a wilderness or here at home, I am here to serve You. Lead me to others today. You truly are great and awesome! I lift my love to You!

---

by Tonya Mechling

Remembering God at 11:48 p.m.

After almost exactly 24 months since I started praying for it, at about 3 p.m. that day, I got it. The *it* is not relevant to the telling of the story. Even though in all those months I had lost neither faith nor hope, I was surprised and breathtakingly delighted at finally getting it.

First, I texted my husband with the good news.

Then I told my kids.

Third, I called my parents and my mother-in-law.

Finally, I sat down to make a list of friends to email about the news—since so many had been praying for me.

To top off my good day with more goodness, Roy got take-out from Olive Garden and gave me a break from the kitchen that evening.

I could not have asked for a better day. The usual streak of bad luck that creeps in at the 11th hour missed my door altogether that day. Curling up with Mr. Kitty, I watched a movie in bed and smiled to myself.

Almost midnight, I turned off the lights, slipped under the covers, feeling very blessed and content. And only then did I remember. In all my elation, I had forgotten to thank God!

I was ashamed. So many years, so many miracles, so many awesome gifts later, I can still be such a brat.

So I turned on the lights to blog about my self-centered day, to stop and give thanks to the God who gave me that day and that wonderful answer to 24 months of praying.

Promise yourself to end each day thanking God for something specific that happened to you. Even on the worst day, if you think really hard, I bet you'll find something for which to be thankful.

---

by Fylvia Fowler Kline

Lessons From My Hot Tub

1. The colder the weather, the hotter my tub needs to be. When I am surrounded by people and circumstances that shake and test my faith, I need to make sure my time with the Lord is sufficient to withstand the influences around me.

2. No matter how much my muscles and joints hurt, when I get in the hot tub, I feel good. When I am with God, all the hurts of life go away.

3. No matter how frigid the temperature outside, the hot tub refreshes my body. It doesn't matter how bad my sin, God forgives.

4. When I dash to the tub through snow and chilling winds, the water is at first too hot. But very quickly it feels so good and just right. When God is trying to teach me, it doesn't always feel comfortable at first. But staying right with Him, I eventually appreciate the lessons I've learned.

5. Parts of my body that are not immersed in the heat of the hot tub can feel the snow and icy rain blowing on my face and hair. While this can diminish my enjoyment of the hot tub, my aches and pains still benefit. In the hardest experiences

of life when I think that God has given up on me and doesn't care, putting myself in a place where He can surround me with His love and warmth will bring me through the experience with less pain and heartache.

6. Getting out of the hot tub with wet feet onto the snow and ice covered patio can be a slippery experience. Right after a mountaintop experience with the Lord is when the devil works the hardest to make me fall.

7. Watching the first sunrise from the warmth of the hot tub is awesome, especially after a week of snowy days. Being close to God's warmth enhances my day.

8. The stars are the brightest and most enjoyable on a cold winter's night. No matter what is happening in my life, I can always find joy.

9. My body hurts less when I use the hot tub at least twice a day. My spiritual well-being is greatest when I spend time with God morning and evening.

_____

by Glenda Maxson-Davidson

Something to Crow About

Ah, the lovely sounds of the country. Humming tractors, chickens clucking, peaceful breeze blowing through the trees and the crowing of a rooster.

The rooster at the farm next door started crowing early one morning. I smiled, loving the sound. The second hour of his music, I went outside on my deck to hear it better. The third hour of the noise, I wondered when he was going to stop. By the fifth hour, I was ready to clobber me one big bird. My lovely country music turned into an aggravating, annoying soliloquy of noise!

Does this sound like anyone you know? I'm not a big talker but I can chew my husband's ear off when I have him trapped on the porch swing. I have found myself rambling on and on. My sweet husband may want to smack me on the head, but he just smiles. I know he has had enough when he stands up and stretches. I know then that he wants to go in.

The Bible has a lot to say on what we crow about. Ephesians 5:19 says, *Sing praises over everything, any excuse for a song to God the Father in the name of our Master, Jesus Christ.* By the fourth hour, I was thinking I need to go recite Ephesians 5:4 to the rooster: *Don't talk dirty or silly. That kind of talk doesn't fit our style. Thanksgiving is our dialect.* His singing had turned into foolish, silly talk, as far as I was concerned. I wanted to give him a piece of my mind. Then I had to recite Ephesians 4:29 to myself, *Watch the way you talk. Let nothing foul or dirty come out of your mouth. Say only what helps, each word a gift.*

Ephesians goes on to tell us to get rid of brawling and slander. I wasn't about to go brawling with a rooster and I apologize for slandering him. But the whole episode was a good reminder of my own crowing.

Upon further pondering, I see that maybe I have this rooster all wrong. The Bible says we are to have praise on our lips. The day was gorgeous. Maybe he was just praising. Psalm 145:21 says, *Let everything living bless him.* Okay, maybe that's a little far fetched. But all I'm saying is that perhaps my lesson from the rooster is that my praises should be heard all throughout the day for all to hear.

After all, God's goodness is something to crow about!

---

by Kristin Bridgman

What's Keeping You up?

For weeks now, I've had a suspicion that I am an addict. To confirm this suspicion, I Googled the signs of addiction: *using the stuff to forget problems or to relax; keeping it a secret; losing interest in activities that used to be important; spending a lot of time figuring out how to get more of it; needing more and more of it.*

I display all these signs. Now I'm certain I am a Wurdle addict. Wurdle is a word game on my iPhone that increases my vocabulary and exercises my brain. Yet, in spite of all its educational value, it is addictive. I find myself Wurdling while on the phone, while sautéing onions, while waiting for the shower to warm up. I even reach for it when I wake up in the middle of a restless night. Wurdle has now virtually replaced my Bible by my bed.

So it's obvious that I need some major intervention — not just for my Wurdle addiction but also for all the other seemingly good stuff that surreptitiously robs my life of time with God. In the Christian life, it is often the good stuff and sinless deeds of a busy life that tempt us away from intimacy with God.

---

by Fylvia Fowler Kline

Katie was My Gift

Katie's mom was not looking forward to another conference that night. Her pinched face said she'd heard enough about how difficult her daughter was in class; how her behavior was disruptive on a daily basis; and how it made learning difficult for the other students. I extended my hand, introduced myself and told her—sincerely—how much I loved having Katie in class.

Her shock was obvious.

Katie was a brilliant and beautiful girl with an enthusiasm for journalism and law. She also had Autism, ADHD and issues with anger management.

I'd heard horror stories from other teachers about her angry rants. One teacher was actually afraid of her. Never having had a student like Katie before, I didn't have any idea of how to handle her.

I quickly noticed that Katie spoke out frequently and had a comment for everything I said. I responded for a while, but realized that she didn't understand when the conversation was over. Had I let it go on, she would have monopolized the entire class. So I looked her in the eye and said firmly, *Katie, I really want to*

hear what you have to say, but now is not the time.
Then, responding to something whispering to me
from somewhere, I asked if she'd like to come back
after school and talk. She looked surprised, yet
somewhat skeptical.

I kept my word. I stayed after school and let her talk
for as long as she wanted. A billion words poured out
of Katie about everything from class to anime to law.
When she finished, she left abruptly. No *See you
tomorrow* or *Goodbye.* She just left.

This became an almost daily occurrence.

Was it wearing me out? You bet. By that time of the
day, I'm exhausted and ready to clean up my
classroom and get on with grading, planning, etc. But
what it did for Katie was just remarkable. It didn't
change her behavior altogether. She still interrupted
constantly, but she never lost her temper in class. She
believed that when I said I'd give her time after
school, I would keep my word. And I did.

She just needed to be *heard.* She needed to believe
that her thoughts mattered to someone.

Katie's mother told me later that I had given her a
priceless gift. I assured her that she had it backwards.
Katie was my gift.

---

by Tess Wigginton

Ready for Fall

Spring brings beauty and warmth to our seasonal cycle of life. The rebirth of plants and animals awakens us to the joys of being renewed ourselves. But have you ever considered fall? The fall colors are glorious in beauty with the mild days that rescue us from hiding inside the air-conditioned heaven we sought from summer's heat.

But I view fall a little differently now as I grow older. As my life on this planet comes to an end, it's too much like the *Fall*.

I have in my front yard a beautiful apple tree. Its branches are full in the spring. But as fall comes on harder each day, the tree shows signs of death of another season. Unharvested apples, filled with spots and decay, fall frequently to the ground. Leaves turn yellow and brown. Rake in hand, I clear the life that is now debris and remember how full of life the tree was just a few months earlier—apple blossoms, with bees swarming for their nectar, filled the whole tree , creating a picture of beauty.

How much like the apple blossom we are. We start off beautiful, maturing on our branch. If we are well taken care of, we resist the insects that invade us and become fruit that nourishes others.

But if I had not cared for my tree with water, fertilizer and pest control, my apples would have been far from nourishing.

As I rake the fallen apples and leaves into a pile and place them in a pile too many to count, I wonder both about my apple tree and my life. How similar is my life to the apple and the fall that is quickly, inevitably approaching? Am I ready to be used in a good way or am I destined for the compost pile?

For the apple tree, I have till next year. For myself, now is a good a time as any.

by Laurie Owen

The Life Guard

Why are you down in the dumps, dear soul? Why are you crying the blues? Fix my eyes on God—soon I'll be praising again. He puts a smile on my face. He's my God. Psalm 42:11

I sulked in the far corner of the swimming pool. There was only one other person in the pool and he was chatting with the lifeguard.

I could drown right here and they wouldn't even notice, I thought. Yes, I can swim. But that wasn't the point. I was just miffed that the lifeguard was so engrossed in conversation that he wasn't paying attention to his job. Of course, I knew the lifeguard was doing his job even if it didn't seem so. It was just my bad attitude rearing its ugly head.

It occurred to me that my frustrations ran deeper than a seemingly negligent lifeguard. The real issue was that I felt God was not paying attention to my needs. But that was just my carnal mind speaking. I know with certainty that the Lord God is watching out for His children at all times regardless of what my tattered emotions say.

Jesus is not just a lifeguard who stands by in case we start to sink. He is always there guarding every part of our lives whether we feel His presence or not. And

He is never negligent! The Bible says to cast all our cares upon Him for He cares for us.

Looking at the lifeguard at the pool again, I chastised and reminded myself that though our Heavenly Father guards our lives, we have a responsibility to guard our thoughts. Rather than letting our downcast emotions rule our thoughts, we must bring them into subjection by praising God!

by Susan Shimkovitz

Farewells Come Quickly

The message read: *Attention—Betty is retiring. Farewell lunch next week*

I've known Betty for five years. She works two cubicles and a corridor from me. If there were a prize for motivation, Betty would win the gold. Velcro'd on her cubicle wall is a new saying every day. Today it's a serious one: *Do not ask for tasks that equal your powers. Instead ask for powers that equal your tasks.* The other day it said, *Life is too short—eat dessert first.*

The angry, the weary, the disheartened and the temporarily insane—they all stop at Betty's. One day, when I was both weary and insane, I stopped at Betty's. *I need to get away from this crazy place. Maybe move to some place quiet. Quit my job. Downsize and live on less,* I blurted exhausted by everything that was going on in my life.

Betty, I'm sure, knew this was just craziness talking. But she did more than listen. The next day she brought me brochures and real estate magazines from tranquil West Virginia. She even brought train schedules and maps to show me how I could keep my job in Maryland and still move to a quiet place. All this she did knowing that a few rational weeks later I would come to my senses and the literature would end up in the trash.

What have I done for Betty in five years? There's nothing I have that she needs—except perhaps my cooking. Betty loves Indian food. Neither fancy nor picky, she is delighted with a reused yogurt container filled with my leftovers. But I'm full of excuses—too late to pack the leftovers; forgot it in the mad morning rush; the leftovers are just enough to stretch for dinner; too many things to carry today.

For as long as I've known Betty, I've taken her for granted. In a couple of weeks Betty will be gone. There's little I can do to fix the past five years. But there's plenty I can do about today and all the tomorrows.

Take five minutes to think about all the things you've been putting off for too long. Then do just one of those today.

---

by Fylvia Fowler Kline

Orchestrated by God

Don't let this throw you. You trust God, don't you? John 14:1

For two weeks we have been counting down to the picnic. My son has autism, but that doesn't stop his love for food, fun and fellowship.

The day was finally here and we were now counting down hours, not days. *Three more hours, two more hours, one more hour and it will be time for the picnic. Yay!* After a quick stop at the library, we hopped in the car to head down the highway. Our windows were down and we were enjoying the breeze and nice weather.

As we approached the ramp I heard a very loud clicking sound. As I accelerated, the sound worsened-- click, click, clack, clack, hissss, hisssss, CLACK! I immediately prayed, *Lord please help us.* My mind raced as I took the next turn. I knew I had few options and being stuck on the side of the road with a child who doesn't understand emergencies wasn't one of them.

So I pressed on slowly at 20 miles per hour with my hazard lights. The tire was going flat fast on the passenger's side.

Lord what should I do? Do I keep going? Stop? Take a detour and find a repair shop?

Cars began speeding past us as we kept driving very slowly. And then, suddenly, a church member pulled up beside us and offered help!

Only God can orchestrate all of the little things to play out like it did that day. Of the hundreds of cars on the road at that time, God sent the right person at the right time to help us. Everything worked out perfectly—the car was dropped off at the repair shop while we attended the picnic.

What a fun picnic it was, and my son never knew that anything was really wrong. Later, when we went to pick up the car, the folks there waived the service fee. I choked up, my eyes welled with tears and I rejoiced in the goodness of the Lord.

---

by Delicia Barrow

Jumpstart

Suddenly, GOD, you floodlight my life; I'm blazing with glory, God's glory! I smash the bands of marauders, I vault the highest fences.
Psalm 18:28, 29

Some people drink coffee to get their day started. Some have energy drinks. Others may get their day going with an invigorating run. I have a verse for you that will jumpstart your day. Cast aside your usual morning pick-me-ups and open your Bible to Psalm 18:28, 29.

David wrote this Psalm when God delivered him from Saul. I see David running upon troops and leaping over walls and being inspired to write of his experience. God had given him the strength he needed to do the work God called him to do. God surely gives us the strength we need for each day too.

We all have stories of God giving us miraculous feats of strength. Mine happened last year when my husband fractured his clavicle in a motorcycle escapade. Being a non-motorcycle person, I cannot really explain how one becomes trapped under a motorcycle dangling from a large truck. I heard my husband call my name from out in the driveway one evening. I rushed out, barefooted, to see him trapped under his heavy bike. I only had time to call for help from on high. I knew that there was no way that I could lift the bike. My husband's head was smashed into the pavement, yet he calmly said, *Tonya, lift the bike off of me.*

Without questions or hesitation, I reached down and lifted the heavy beast off of my husband. I did not even feel the weight of the bike. I know some unseen hands wrapped around mine and lifted the 250-pound bike off of my husband.

For by You I can run upon a troop; And by my God I can leap over a wall (NKJ). I do not know what troops, walls or bikes you will encounter today, but I do know that God will empower you with the mental and physical arsenal you need to do the job. Praise Him for His wonderful works in your life today!

---

by Tonya Mechling

Free at Last

Absolutely everything, ranging from small to large, as you make it a part of your believing prayer, gets included as you lay hold of God. Matthew 21:22

After going to church through a dare, I finally found what I had been looking for in all the wrong places.

I found the love of God and I wanted to be one of His children. My next step was to learn more about Him through His Word. I had scorned the Bible before, but now I found it to be a great treasure. After a couple of meetings with the pastor, my conviction grew stronger. But at every step there was a stumbling block of some triviality or another.

Just as I was really getting into studying my Bible, I came home one day to discover that my well-behaved dog had torn my marked Bible into a million pieces.

Next, just a few days before I was to be baptized, I came down with a bad case of strep throat. My fever was so high that I began to hallucinate. The day before the baptism the pastor came to visit. Seeing how sick I was, he suggested postponing it. But there was no way I was going to delay my decision to declare my new freedom in Jesus.

The next day at church it was discovered that the baptismal water heater was not working. The water was frigidly cold. But even that was not going to change my mind.

I didn't hear much of the sermon that preceded the baptism. I was closeted in prayer, anxious about my new life that was about to begin. When it was time, I moved to the changing room to get ready. Just then the same elder who told me about the broken water heater excitedly reported that the water in the baptismal tank was warm!

It was my little miracle. It was my God reminding me that as long as I persevered in following Him and as long as I loved Him more and more each day, He would be there for me.

When I was submerged in the baptismal water, I felt Jesus break the chains of Satan, the ones I had worn for so long. When I came out of the water, I was finally free at last!

_____

by Vicky Tibbetts

Every Woman's Dream

This old journal entry says a lot about how I've managed to stay married :)

What girl has not dreamt of one day meeting the perfect man, the one especially created for you, the husband with whom you will live happily ever after. I was no different. I wanted a Good-Morning-I-love-you-Honey, Rockwellian life. Instead I got a husband whose most affectionate term of endearment is *Yo.*

Yes, I got myself a man who uses a variation of the dog whistle to get my attention in public; who takes hours to teach our children the art of burping the alphabet; who scratches himself in inappropriate places at inappropriate times. And I am latched to him for the rest of my life in spite of his crass jokes and well-bitten fingernails that grate me like chalk on a writing board.

At night I close my eyes shut while he snorts in my ear and straddles his heavy leg over my waist and I dream of a Good-Morning-I-Love-you-Honey life that passed me by. And it takes a day like today to realize just how lucky I am.

Well actually it started yesterday. The house was a big mess and needed a thorough cleaning. My mother-in-law was coming to spend a couple of days with us. I was tired and my back was sore. By 9 p.m. I had done all I could and there was plenty still to be done.

That's when he stepped in and cleaned and cleaned to the music of the Fifth Dimension, the Bee Gees and several others. He whistled, sang along, cracking a few of his prized off-colored jokes in between. Never complained, never threw a fit. Never said *What's this doing here?* or *If only everyone would put things back where they belong!* or any of the other stuff I often say when I clean.

He went on till one in the morning. When I woke up at six, he was already up, putting on some final touches.

I took his nail-bitten hands and kissed them.

Life has not passed me by after all. It's there—all of it. I just have to read between the lines.

---

by Fylvia Fowler Kline

Miscarriage

Like so many other women, I know too well the pain of losing an unborn child. Whether it's in the second month or the sixth, the loss is unbearable and the recovery long.

My first pregnancy ended in miscarriage and although it was extremely difficult for me, it also brought answers. The doctors discovered my problem wasn't in getting pregnant, but in staying that way. My body didn't naturally produce enough of a certain hormone required to sustain the growth and delivery of a baby. Because of this problem, every pregnancy I had would end in miscarriage if I did not begin taking hormone supplements immediately.

The next two times I became pregnant, I began taking the supplements needed to create an environment conducive to fostering the healthy growth, development and delivery of the baby. Both times I delivered fully developed, strong babies—the first time a son, the second identical twin daughters.

Had I chosen not to listen to my doctors and kept trying on my own, I would not have my children today. Isn't it similar in our spiritual lives as well? So many times we are pregnant with promise, only to have its potential aborted because we didn't do our part.

Instead of supplementing our lives with prayer and His Word, we just keep doing things on our own. And because we don't naturally produce faith, peace, longsuffering, gentleness and the other fruits on our own, we need an infusion from Him—daily supplements of His grace and ability to foster the growth and delivery of those things He has promised.

How many blessings have I miscarried because I didn't do my part? Sometimes it requires a lifestyle change. Sometimes spiritual bed rest is what's needed. Whatever it is, in the end, it is worth doing what God expects of us. For to hold His gift, the fulfillment of promise, is infinitely more precious than anything I am asked to give up.

_____

by Deidra Manning

A Little Pick-Me-Up

'Celebrate with me! I found my lost coin!' Count on it—that's the kind of party God's angels throw every time one lost soul turns to God. Luke 15:10

Walking through the parking lot, my son stooped to pick up a coin. *Cool, it's a dime,* he said. *If it had been a penny I wouldn't have bothered.*

I guess he doesn't know that a 1943-D copper cent was recently sold for $1.7 million or that certain other pennies have sold for as much as $200,000 in recent years. Then again, I have no right to talk. There have been many times when I've been too tired, lazy, or busy to bother picking up a stray penny.

If people were coins, Jesus would consider every dull old penny as valuable as a shiny new gold piece. And He would search for every lost penny.

I believe Heaven rejoices when I stop to pick someone up because that is a reflection of Jesus' heart. I pray that I never cease to recognize the value in every human life. After all, everyone could use a little pick-me-up now and then!

---

by Susan Shimkovitz

Empty Shoes

*Honesty lives confident and carefree, but Shifty is sure to be exposed.
Proverbs 10:9*

The little boy sat fidgeting. He moved from his seat
to the empty ones around him. His mother had to
keep pulling him back. Finally, he gave up, took his
shoes off, and curled up next to his mother. I guess he
thought he had no use for shoes if he couldn't get
down and move around. He chose to give up, which
in this instance was probably a good thing since he
was in church.

Jesus asks us to walk in His shoes. He wants us to
walk His way to lead us to a better place. Yet we
often say no and choose our own path in life, whether
it is comfortable or not! We prefer to remain in our
unfulfilling lives. In other words, we give up!

The shoes that Jesus gives us are always a good fit.
The trouble is we won't know how perfect they are
until we try them on. Just like the little boy who
kicked off his shoes because he no longer felt a need
for them, we also sometimes discard the ways of
Jesus for our own.

---

by Patricia Day

The Snickerdoodle Dilemma

I have a sweet tooth. Actually I have a whole set of sweet teeth.

I had just had a heavy lunch, topped off with three large pieces of Belgian chocolate. Armed with more than the recommended daily sugar allowance, I was ready for the second half of my workday. But that was until I stopped at Sheri's desk. Sitting on the counter was a see-through, smell-through bag of Snickerdoodles.

Mmmm—memories of baking with my dad wafted cinnamon aromas into my brain cells.

You must have some, urged my evil dessert twin who lives between the folds of my middle-aged belly.

Maybe just one, I responded, vowing to myself that it was going to be a memorable moment—just my Snickerdoodle and me. I resolved to eat it slowly, relishing each little bite. Instead, like a dog head to head with a pound of meat, I snarled and stuffed the cookie into my drooling mouth. It was quite an indecent spectacle—right there in the office hallway!

175

I didn't stop to appreciate the snickerdoodly lightness or enjoy the cinnamony sugar granules. It was just a greedy, self-serving three-step process: gnaw, drool, swallow. I didn't even chew that worthy Snickerdoodle.

And before it could get down my throat—I wanted more. I turned around and went back. Complimenting Sheri on her baking skills, I apologetically said, *I have to have another.* She graciously encouraged me to take a handful.

I'm going to enjoy these, I promised myself, truly believing that I had total self-control. But just as the cookie got closer to my mouth, it was another gnaw, drool and swallow.

Five minutes and several cookies later, I felt the thick, sweet, nasty aftertaste of Snickerdoodles. Funny, how I had forgotten that sickening, awful aftertaste. Somehow I remembered only the initial joy of biting into one.

Life has many Snickerdoodles. Like the excessive alcohol that mixes a great evening with friends for a sensation of well being. But then comes the nasty hangover the morning after. Or the other little self indulgent moments that return to haunt us.

What are we to do with our Snickerdoodles?!

———————————————

by Fylvia Fowler Kline

Squeezing the Sponge

When the pressure builds up, what's stored in your heart and mind is squeezed to the surface. It's easy to say and do just the right things when all is well, but when the pressure builds up and chaos takes over, who you really are deep down within comes to the surface.

It's like squeezing a sponge.

At the end of a big cleaning day, there are sponges to testify to all the work that was done. Sometimes, however, you lose track of which sponge was used for what purpose. But squeezing it usually gives you a clue.

You pick up the first sponge and squeeze it over the sink. A brown fluid drips out and you remember the bottle of Pepsi that spilled. Out of another sponge flows out bubbly disinfectant; that was used to clean the bathroom. A third sponge exudes a definite smell of motor oil from the garage. The last drips yellowish, pine-scented Pine-Sol; that was definitely used on the kitchen floor.

To look at, they're all the same. Only squeezing sets them apart.

Our lives are like sponges. On the surface we all are pretty similar in our polite, courteous public images. But underneath all that, what has really been soaked up inside? If you were squeezed, what would your heart reveal?

Whether the squeeze is physical, emotional, mental or spiritual, it reveals your true strength and character. Do you lash out in anger or do you respond with love and patience? Do ugly words spill out or do you take a deep breath and remember that you've been on the other side many a time? Do you resort to revenge or do you choose to forgive?

Just like a sponge that only drips what it has been soaked with, fill yourself with things pleasing to the Lord. Read God's Word, pray often, spend positive time with others. Soak up all that's good. And when the pressure builds, it'll drip back into your life to strengthen and give you peace.

by Jennifer Shelton

Insurance vs. Assurance

You know well enough how the wind blows this way and that. You hear it rustling through the trees, but you have no idea where it comes from or where it's headed next. John 3:8

The winds were fierce at my Kentucky home that morning. I love hearing the great sounds of thunder and watching lightning streak across the sky. It reminds me of growing up in the tornado alleys of Oklahoma.

The devastating destruction of tornado winds can pop up so quickly and take unexpected turns, just like the winds of life. You may think you know which direction you're headed, but when the winds kick up unexpectedly and change course quickly, you can be knocked off your feet.

If a tree falls on your roof, you have insurance. But what happens when the winds of life strike you down?

For that, there's something better than insurance— God's assurance. *He told the wind to pipe down and said to the sea, 'Quiet! Settle down! The wind ran out of breath; the sea became smooth as glass. (Mark 4:39). When you're in over your head, I'll be there*

179

with you. When you're in rough waters, you will not go down (Isaiah 43:2).

We are not promised a life without storms. Yet, we need not fear or be alarmed. When the howling, blowing winds come across your path, stand strong knowing God is near.

During my last life storm, I began to sink like Peter on the water when he took his eyes off Jesus. But when I turned my focus back on my Savior, I was able to fight. I clung to His promise: *Don't panic. I'm with you. There's no need to fear for I'm your God. I'll give you strength. I'll help you. I'll hold you steady, keep a firm grip on you (Isaiah 41:10).*

Insurance covers only some things. But God's assurance covers everything. Plus, it's free with no premiums to pay!

_____

by Kirstin Bridgman

Faith in a Box

In the first ten minutes, it was quite obvious he had thoroughly Googled me. Not in the creepy, stalker kind of way; but in an I-better-know-whom-I-might-be-working-with, smart sort of way. So when he said *Tell me about yourself,* it was just as obvious that he wasn't talking about my work experience, my portfolio, my rambling blog or even my penchant for chocolate.

What more was there to say about me that wasn't already plastered online? So, I told the truth. And in telling the truth, I broke every rule there is on job interviews: keep separate business and personal, emotions and knowledge, personal faith and professional career.

I said, *First and foremost, I am a woman of faith.*

As soon as the words were out, I realized they would either make or break the deal. And the realization washed over me with pride—yes, pride; not regret. In that moment, I realized that my life really is one big box of everything.

There are no compartments to my soul or persona. I am the same person at home and at work. Sure, most of the time, I have the sense to know what to keep to myself and when to shut up. But when it comes down to what makes me tick, what steers my choices, what makes my relationships, what sets my priorities, what forms my work ethic and my integrity, it is my faith.

And faith is one thing that absolutely cannot be compartmentalized. It cannot be kept in an exclusive box of its own.

---

by Fylvia Fowler Kline

Not Yet

Everyone who calls, 'Help, God!' gets help. Romans 10:13

There were about 30 of us picnicking along Pack River. My oldest daughter, Tonya, was about four or five years old. She had long, thick blond hair that, even after I pulled up in a ponytail and divided into six thick braids, reached her waist. She wanted to join the other children in the water. Since the river was very shallow, we said yes.

As I stood on the bank of the river watching Tonya, she suddenly disappeared! All I could see were six braids floating on the water's surface. I froze. I couldn't speak. Finally, after what seemed like hours, I pointed and yelled for her. My father-in-law heard me and jumped into the water. Grabbing the blond braids, he pulled Tonya up and above the water. In a panic, I reached out to grab her from his arms. To my surprise, he wouldn't give her to me. *Not yet,* he said as he headed back to the water with Tonya.

Together they walked back into the water. They began to splash and play and giggle.

I was grateful that the incident did not create a fear of water in Tonya. Yet, for years, every once in a while when I'd shampoo her long hair, she would shake and gasp for air. The memory of that incident in the river was buried in her subconscious, but the healing that came from facing the water again with her grandpa had wiped away any long-term, debilitating damage.

My father-in-law's words, *Not yet,* were a valuable lesson to me.

We often find ourselves under water and alone. And when God rescues us, the experience becomes our strength to survive other dangers. Not only does God keep us safe, but He also equips us to face whatever life may throw our way.

---

by Vicky Tibbetts

My Blue Bird and Me

Merlin, my blue and gold macaw, and I have been together for 13 years. The beauty and intelligence with which God created him amaze me—he talks in full sentences, solves problems, figures out creative ways to do things.

Over the years, Merlin and I have bonded so strongly that it's very difficult to leave him in someone else's care when I am out of town. When we are reunited, he is so happy to see me; yet he scolds me to let me know he did not like being left with someone else.

I am the only mother Merlin has known. When he was a baby, I fed him Cheerios with a spoon. An adult bird now, Merlin has the maturity of a three-year-old human. And just like a toddler, he has temper tantrums and fears. When he senses danger, he nervously screams for me from wherever he is. Immediately, I reassure him with cuddles and coos until he calms down. Merlin and I also spend a lot of quality time together. I've spent long hours teaching him games and tricks like peek-a- boo, catch and high five.

I find it very interesting that he does his tricks without expecting rewards; he simply wants to please me. Like a person, there is beauty as well as flaws in him. While his plumes are gorgeously bright and colorful, he can be quite messy when eating or preening himself.

I imagine God looks at both the good and not so good in me and loves me just the same, just as I do Merlin. I understand Merlin's limitations just as God understands the sin that handicaps me.

God looks at the messes in my life and cleans it all up. Not once, but over and over again.

---

by Laurie Owen

Cleanliness and Godliness

If the statement *Cleanliness is next to godliness* were true, we'd be in trouble! Forget about the piles of laundry, dirty dishes in the sink and toilets that need scrubbing. Think about the spiritual mess in all of us.

Sin is like the buildup on my hand mirror. Applying makeup and styling hair every day results in a buildup of dust and hair spray. It happens so gradually that I grow accustomed to the distorted view and continue using the same mirror day after day without noticing the barrier that is building up between my reflection and me. Eventually it becomes so bad that something must be done. And every time I clean it, I'm amazed at how much more clearly I can see my reflection. Then I wonder how I ever used it with all that gunk on it.

In the same way, sin builds up and gradually creates a barrier between God and us. It's so gradual, we don't realize how it slowly deteriorates our relationship with God. The good news is that cleanup is easy. *If we admit our sins—make a clean breast of them—He won't let us down; He'll be true to himself. He'll forgive our sins and purge us of all wrongdoing.*

(1 John 1:9). It doesn't matter how much sin distorts our view of God. He can clean it up. *If your sins are blood-red, they'll be snow-white (Isaiah 1:18).*

When our life mirror is clean, our relationship with God will be pure. So yes, cleanliness is next to godliness.

---

by Tresa Walker

Animal Cracker Personality Test

I'm standing in the parking lot wondering why I had just purchased a giant bag of animal crackers. No exaggeration, it's huge. Three pounds! It has been 10 years or more since I've supported a child with a need of a constant supply of animal crackers. So why did I just blow $3.78 on this?

There's nothing like a good self-analysis. So I sit in my car, refusing to leave the parking lot until I figure out why I had just done what I did.

Like all good shrinks, I begin tracing my emotional link to animal crackers through a series of questions: *Of what did they remind me? Is one animal shape particularly more painful to remember another? Do images of mutilated cracker animals keep me up all night? Have I experienced some kind of separation anxiety that's acutely tied to these crackers?*

Well, the questioning works. Here's my analysis: The big giant red bag of animal crackers represents the big giant hole in my momminess. Grabbing it was symbolic of me yearning to reach into the past and get back the memory-making era when my children were growing up–little people on their way to being grownups. The animal crackers made me remember how, even as little kids, each was a unique individual. And the way they ate their animal crackers told me so much about each one:

Kenny would grab a handful out of the jar and throw them into his mouth one after the other, ball-in-hoop style. Jez would sort his crackers by kinds of animals and then proceed to eat one animal group at a time. Sky would bite off heads and limbs and throw the limbless, headless bodies back in the cookie jar!

At 120 calories per 16 animal crackers, it's going to be at least a hundred days before I eat all of them. I guess I might as well make the most of it—I shall remember more fun things from my mommy days as I bite off cracker limbs.

---

by Fylvia Fowler Kline

The Family Legacy

I don't recall the program. I cannot remember his name. But I was blessed. The speaker was well educated with a plethora of degrees listed after his name. Obviously well known and well traveled, his speech was articulate and fluent. My hand lingered over the radio dial. There was something in his voice. I was eager to hear more.

He spoke of his humble roots. The family had been very poor. It was a tale filled with discrimination and rejection. In a scenario where most would have given up, he chose to make his story different. There was pride in his voice as he spoke of his family legacy. He regaled his audience with musings from his past. Against the odds, his family built a legacy of which they were proud. His was a home where character and integrity meant more than worldly possessions.

As I listened, my thoughts wandered to my own family legacy. I immediately thought of the huckleberry patch in the Idaho wilderness where I picked berries with my grandparents each summer. In that beautiful quiet serene place, my grandparents shared Jesus with me. I will always cherish those times. This summer as I picked berries in the same huckleberry patch from 20 years ago, I was reminded

191

of my heritage. My parents and grandparents gifted me with an incredible legacy of Christian love.

We each have family traditions and customs that are passed down, but we are also part of a greater family legacy. *All these pioneers who blazed the way, all these veterans cheering us on? It means we'd better get on with it. Strip down, start running—and never quit!* (Hebrews 12:1). Jesus is coming again, and we have hope through the examples of our brothers and sisters in Christ through the ages. We truly are the family of God!

---

by Tonya Mechling

The P Word

Don't fret or worry. Instead of worrying, pray. Let petitions and praises shape your worries into prayers. Phil. 4:6

For 16 years I dreaded opening the phone bill. Every time, it brought with it anxiety, guilt, fear, questions and arguments.

Yesterday was no different. 800 dollars! I asked David about the calls yet again. His answer was the same, *I didn't make them. You must have.*

It began 16 years ago, a few weeks after I returned home from the hospital with my newborn. I noticed two unrecognizable numbers in the phone bill. They were calls made when I was in the hospital and there was no one home. (David was out of town when I had my baby.) I called the numbers. To my horror, I reached a pornography service!

Months later, I learned that David was at home while I was in the hospital having our baby! David denied everything and I began my roller coaster ride of guilt. *What was wrong with me? Wasn't I a good wife? Wasn't I pretty enough? Didn't I fulfill my wifely duties? Didn't I maintain a good home? Was I too heavy? Too thin? The wrong shape? Not smart enough?* There was no end to my questions. Along with the guilt was the fear of discovery by family, church and friends.

The months turned into years. Besides the phone calls, there were magazines and movies. I tried everything, but there was no change in David. Finally, after 16 years, I left him.

I turned to God in prayer and sought counseling. Slowly I began to understand that the addiction was David's and that I was not responsible for it. I learned that God could make my life new again, free from guilt.

P may be for pornography, but it also is for prayer. When I was able to completely stop dwelling on the wrong *P* and focus on the right *P,* I was able to move on with my life.

My faith continues to deepen as I learn more about God and His love. His commandments in Exodus 20:3-17 are not burdensome (1 John 5:2,3). Christ has set us free from our burdens (Gal. 5:1). I also continue to pray for the addiction to be taken away from David and that he will be free.

All things are possible through prayer (Matt. 21:22). My prayer for you is that you too will receive peace through your prayers.

---

by Tammy Gray

Mismatched Forever

Roy and I are as dissimilar a couple you can find. We neither share interests nor agree on anything. And 20 some years of marriage have failed to make any progress towards compatibility. Roy's the guy on the very tip of the farthest end from the other guy who remembers his woman's favorite restaurant and color and who ends phone conversations with "Love you."

I could list 100 annoying things about him in five minutes flat. Yet there are about 10 other things he does as father and husband that totally tip the scale.

1.   Assigns himself all poop jobs that gross me out— diapers, litter box, vomit, etc.

2.   Creates rituals that breed warm, fuzzy feelings— makes his special stash of coffee just for Jez, every weekend; places a bar of dark Godiva on my pillow on random evenings; gives Sky no occasion gifts of antique knick-knacks.

3.   Talks to the pets in a silly baby voice that turns them into silly Jell-O creatures.

4.   Covers and tucks me in throughout the night. (I kick the sheets off and then curl up feeling cold.)

5. Calls my mother every Thursday.

6. Keeps my kitchen sink free of dirty dishes. (He's quite OCD with this one. The moment an empty cup hits the counter, it's gone without the slightest chance of being reused. But, enough said; this is not the list of annoying habits.)

7. Saves every piece of family memorabilia—all my published work, the children's crafts and even an antler the dog brought home 15 years ago. (I, on the other hand, have yet to work on my firstborn's baby book. He turned 27 this year.)

8. Fills my car with gas. (Like a ninja, he disappears every now and then and my car is magically never on empty.)

9. Makes a signature peanut butter sandwich. (He can't heat leftovers, but the ritual and memories of his peanut butter sandwiches have earned him a trophy from the kids. Even as adults, they ask him to fix them some.)

10. Trusts me completely. (If we were millionaires, I could easily take all the money and elope with the chauffeur and he wouldn't see it coming.)

Make someone feel special today. Write them a note listing at least three things you appreciate about them.

———————————————————————

by Fylvia Fowler Kline

Meet the Contributors

Joy Alexander. Using my gifts of music, leading worship services, and writing is how I bring my alabaster box to Jesus' feet. The box is filled with triumphs and tragedies, sadness and service; but most of all it's filled with hope that tomorrow will always be a better day. *page 40*

Delicia Barrow. As I journey through life, God is always with me, teaching me to trust Him in all things and to take one day at a time. Every day I grow closer and closer to Him. Without Him I am nothing. *page 163*

Rose McCormick Brandon. I write from personal experiences and contribute to several publications, including The Testimony, The Evangel and Chicken Soup for the Soul. My latest book, *One Good Word Makes all the Difference,* was published in 2013. My husband, Doug, and I live in Caledonia, Ontario. *rosemccormickbrandon.wordpress.com, page 120*

Kristin Bridgman. For many years, I was quiet and confined to my comfort zone. Then God coaxed me out of my shell and into serving others through my blanket ministry for the homeless. God also led me to start a blog where I share my trials and victories. I wear bunny slippers, drink too much tea and ponder way too much. *ponderingsbykris.blogspot.com, pages 24, 84, 152 and 179*

Lyndelle Chiomenti. When I'm not editing the *Collegiate Quarterly Bible Study Guide,* you can find me doing one of the following: gardening, reading, crocheting, dreaming of winning an Olympic gold in figure skating or my absolute favorite—doing pet therapy with my dog, Timmer. *page 8*

Sharon Claassen. I am wife to a wonderful husband and mother to three amazing kids. I have rediscovered my love for writing and combine it with my passion for Christ. *sharonstimewithgod.blogspot.com, page 56*

Cherilyn Clough. In an environment of spiritual and emotional abuse, I grew up afraid of God. But that fear turned to joy when I got to know and love Jesus. I live in Southern Oregon with my husband of 24 years and two cats. I enjoy painting, writing and studying local history. My passion is to share my stories of my wondrous God. *cherilynclough.com, page 110*

Patricia Day. Wrong choices damaged me in many ways and hurt my loved ones. But God's awesome grace and mercy led me to a new life where I share my testimony to help those going through emotional traumas. To read more of my writings, check out my book, *A Stolen Childhood, Eleanor's Story.*
patriciaday.wordpress.com, pages 73, 10, and 174

Tammy Gray. I grew up in a small town close to Vancouver, WA. Every day I remember I am the clay and God is the potter. I pray that with His help I will always be a shining vessel for Him. *page 193*

Doina Jeffery. *page 38*

Amanda Johnson. I am a freelance writer and the assistant editor for *Ruby for Women*, an online Christian women's magazine. I live on a horse farm in rural New England. I am currently building my own ministry of inspirational writings and photography at *foreverinhim.com. pages 46, 98 and 136*

Brenda Kis. I'm just an ordinary woman enjoying this ride of life! Wife, mom, grandma, friend, traveler, recruiter at Adventist Frontier Missions, small group leader, lover of beauty, passionate about almost everything—especially my wonderful God and His Word! *page 102*

Fylvia Fowler Kline. Life has dumped on me like a soap opera. And in the experiencing of it, I've learned that it's much easier letting God be in control. No matter what the drama, I come up stronger, happier and a better person. Most of the episodes I gladly share; others are best left between God and me. *pages 4, 12, 20, 26, 34, 44, 52, 60, 68, 75, 82, 88, 96, 106, 114, 122, 130, 138, 144, 148, 154, 161, 169, 175, 181, 189 and 193.*

Ramona Levacy. My husband, two cats and my job are very rewarding, but my life wouldn't be complete without my writing. I love blogging and am grateful for the power of communication through the Internet. I think of each post as an act of faith, never knowing who might stumble upon my writing and be blessed. *goodchristianfiction.wordpress.com, page 64*

Deidra Manning. I'm a faith blogger, freelance writer, wife and stay-at-home mother of three. I write about life from the middle—of the country, of His grace, of my mess. I'm grateful, I'm hopeful, and I'm blessed. *deidramanning.net, pages 28, 71, 90, 124 and 171*

Mary Maxson. The personal mission given to me by God is to disciple people with the passion of Jesus. I desire to walk beside those who are hurting spiritually, emotionally and physically—and bathe them with prayer. The joy of my life is being called *Nana* by my grandson. *page 58*

Glenda Maxson-Davidson. My walk with God has had its ups and downs, but the unshakable love of God has always centered me. His abundant love pulls me back when I begin to give in to overwhelming burdens of life. Writing helps me process the lessons of the moment and has become an expression of my growing discipleship. *pages 79 and 150*

Tonya Mechling. I am teacher, sister, daughter and friend. Whatever my role or endeavor, God is alive in my life! It is so exciting to see Him work, and I strive to shine for Him each day. Through life's changes, I am continuously reminded of God's promise to me,

Do not fear, for I have redeemed you; I have called you by name; you are Mine (Jeremiah 43:1). pages 6, 112, 128, 146, 165, and 191

Valarie DeLaVega Morse. page 86

Laurie Owen. I am living a life full of love and laughter, sharing the Word with everyone and starting a new life with the husband of my dreams. I am blessed beyond belief and I praise the Lord for His love and mercy every day. pages 10, 42, 108, 132, 157 and 185

Sharon Patterson. I began writing at 30 and was finally published at 60. I write from my triumphs over adversity and soul wounds. I am the author of three books and contributing author for Chicken Soup for the Soul. I live in Round Rock, TX with my husband Garry. page 66

Shianna Paxton. Growing up in a small northwest town, in a rigid, conservative Christian environment, didn't prepare me for the big, cruel world. But when I fell off of God's narrow path, I learned my lesson well and with His help I will never stray again. page 18

Jennifer Shelton. I am the daughter of the Living God, a wife to my best friend and mother to seven blessings. I am taking one day at a time, opening my heart to life lessons from my Creator and using them to bring God glory and strengthen my walk with Him. Where I am weak, He makes me strong.
myrefiningprocess.blogspot.com, page 177

201

Susan Shimkovitz. My childhood was the essence of horror stories. I learned to hate life at a very early age. But I have been able to move past that because God has shown me true love. He has given to me beauty for ashes, the oil of joy for mourning, the garment of praise for the spirit of heaviness; that I might be called a tree of righteousness (Isaiah 61:3). *polishedpearls.wordpress.com, pages 30, 92, 134, 159 and 173*

Beth Steffanaik. A marriage and family counselor for 20 years, I recently transitioned to a certified life coach. My interest in refinishing furniture also reflects how I help others strip away layers of pain so God's love can penetrate and shine through with new and redeemed beauty. Between ministry, motherhood, and mayhem, I blog. *messymarriage.com, page 48*

Amanda Stephan. I'm a homeschooling Christian fiction author. I love to read, review books and create all kinds of crafts. My friends call me Squirrel because I get sidetracked so quickly:) I'm passionate about my relationship with Jesus Christ. *booksbyamanda.com, page 54*

Alvina Kullu Sulankey. I am a teacher and a mother of two. I work and live in beautiful, exotic Thailand. There have been many exciting and some not-so-exciting adventures. As I look back, I realize it was the not-so-exciting ones that brought me closer to Christ. If not for these, my life would have been quite ordinary. *pages 16 and 100*

Ruth-Ann Thompson. From the time I knew that paper and pencil made words and sentences, I have both understood and appreciated the wonderful gift that God has granted me. He saw me lying in an open field and said to me, *Live (Ezekiel 16:4-6)*. And I am grateful that He brought me from the orphanage to the parsonage. *pages 50 and 140*

Vicky Tibbetts. As a nurse, the suffering I encountered every day in the hospital only reinforced my belief that there was no God. But when I met Jesus on a dare, everything changed. Besides being a nurse for 36 years, I have been a logger, a farmer, a law student and a teacher. But most rewarding was the joy of raising four wonderful children. *pages 80, 118, 167 and 183)*

Debra Torres. I'm a wife and a stay-at-home mother to an active brood of five. In my spare time I blog and offer freelance copywriting and web design services. *mychristiandevotionalblog.com, debratorrescopywriter.com, page 142*

Heather Joy Vires. *pages 32, 77 and 116*

Tresa Walker. Writing has been a journey of obedience and blessings through which God gently reminds me that He doesn't expect me to be perfect, just willing. My days are filled with family, teaching fourth grade, leading a women's Bible study and squeezing in some writing. *strengthrenewed.wordpress.com, page 187*

Kathy Walling. I'm grateful for all the goodness in my life and for being able to share with others the joy, love, peace and fellowship that comes from Jesus. *page 14*

Cynthia Ward. I enjoy living in Southern Oregon where I am employed at a small private school. Dealing with a variety of adults and children every day gives me plenty of material for my musings. God has blessed me with a great family and amazing friends who are my support system. *pages 22, 69, 94 and 126*

Cathy Watt. Life is full of honest work, ever-evolving family, close friends, and a sweet dog named Dino. Many lessons have been learned along the way, the most important that good judgment comes from experience, and experience generally comes from bad judgment. I find that every day I am gifted with the blessings of friendship and the grace of forgiveness. *page 6*

Tess Wigginton. I have never been satisfied with easy answers. Looking deeper comes as naturally to me as breathing or eating. My faith is far too complex to be contained; therefore I search endlessly for a system that defines what I feel in my entire being. I know that it surrounds me and runs through me. If only I could give it a name. *deepbluenight.wordpress.com,* *pages 36 and 155*

.

www.ingramcontent.com/pod-product-compliance
Lightning Source LLC
LaVergne TN
LVHW011154080426
835508LV00007B/405